NERO

WHO WAS...

NERO

The Singing Emperor

NOONIE MINOGUE

Illustrations by Alex Fox

✷ SHORT BOOKS

First published in 2005 by
Short Books
15 Highbury Terrace
London N5 1UP

10 9 8 7 6 5 4 3 2 1

A CIP catalogue record for this book
is available from the British Library.

Illustration copyright © Alex Fox 2005
Quiz by Sebastian Blake

ISBN 1-904977-11-1

Printed in Great Britain by
Bookmarque Ltd., Croydon, Surrey

The Cast

Agrippina (the younger) – mother of Nero, wife of Gnaeus Domitius Ahenobarbus, daughter of the famous general Germanicus and of Agrippina the elder; great grand-daughter of Augustus, neice and then wife of the Emperor Claudius.

Ahenobarbus (Gnaeus Domitius) – father of Nero, grandson of Mark Antony, great nephew of Augustus.

Ahenobarbus (Lucius Domitius) – the name Nero was called until his adoption by Claudius.

Britannicus – son of Claudius and Messalina, brother of Octavia, step-brother of Nero.

Caligula or "little-Boot" (Gaius Caeser) – Emperor 37-41AD, great nephew of Tiberius, brother of Agrippina, Livilla and Drusilla, uncle of Nero.

Claudius – Emperor 41-54AD. Brother of Germanicus, uncle and later, husband of Agrippina. Nero's great-uncle and step-father. Adopted Nero as his own son in 50AD.

Domitia – Nero's eldest aunt, sister of Gnaeus Domitius Ahenobarbus and Lepida; wife of Crispus Passienus until he divorced her and married Agrippina instead.

Lepida – Nero's aunt who took care of him during Agrippina's exile, also mother of Messalina and grandmother of Britannicus.

Messalina – Nero's first cousin. wife of Emperor Claudius, mother of Britannicus and Octavia, forced to commit suicide 48AD.

Octavia – Nero's step-sister, then first wife, divorced and killed at his orders 62AD.

Poppaea – Nero's second wife, previously wife of his friend Otho. Died 65AD.

Tiberius – Nero's great-great uncle, Emperor from 14-37AD.

Other important characters

Acte — Nero's first love, a Greek ex-slave.

Anicetus — A tutor of Nero. Helped Nero to dispose of his mother and wife.

Burrus (Afranius) — Appointed Commander of the Praetorian Guard by Agrippina; Seneca's colleague as tutor and advisor to Nero.

Lucan (Marcus Annaeus) — Seneca's nephew, a poet. Early on, a member of Nero's inner circle, later forced to commit suicide after being named in the conspiracy of Piso.

Petronius (Arbiter) — Supreme judge of elegance, and probable author of a low-life novel in prose and verse called The Satyricon. Named in the Pisonian conspiracy by his enemy Tigellinus, he committed suicide.

Piso (Gaius Calpurnius) — The man who gives his name to a conspiracy against Nero in 65AD which caused 19 executions.

Seneca (Lucius Annaeus) — Nero's tutor, orator, philosopher and famous writer of letters and tragedies. Committed suicide after being named in the conspiracy of Piso 65 AD.

Tigellinus — In 62AD he replaced Burrus as Commander of the Praetorian Guard. A man of 'low birth' and vicious reputation; created a network of informers and secret police and received triumphal honours for his loyalty in the Pisonian conspiracy.

The 3 emperors of 69AD

Galba — Governor of Spain invited by *Vindex* to replace Nero in 68AD.

Otho — Friend of Nero and first husband of Poppaea, Nero's second wife. Sent to govern Lusitania (Portugal) in 58AD.

Vitellius — Another friend of Nero's and a notorious glutton. Emperor from June to December 69AD. When Vespasian's (the next emperor's) army arrived, he tried to escape in a sedan chair with a cook and a pastry chef, but was dragged out of his hiding place, and thrown into the river Tiber.

NERO'S FAMILY

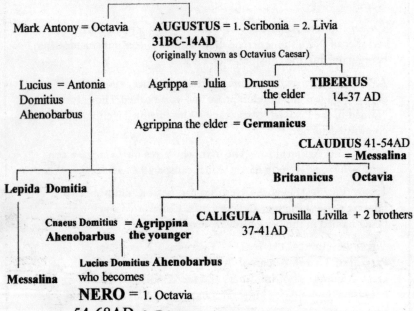

Mark Antony = Octavia   **AUGUSTUS** = 1. Scribonia = 2. Livia
31BC-14AD
(originally known as Octavius Caesar)

Lucius = Antonia   Agrippa = Julia   Drusus   **TIBERIUS**
Domitius   the elder   14-37 AD
Ahenobarbus

Agrippina the elder = **Germanicus**

CLAUDIUS 41-54AD
= **Messalina**

Britannicus   Octavia

Lepida Domitia

Cnaeus Domitius = **Agrippina**   **CALIGULA**   Drusilla Livilla + 2 brothers
Ahenobarbus   the younger   37-41AD

Lucius Domitius **Ahenobarbus**
who becomes

Messalina

NERO = 1. Octavia
54-68AD   2. Poppaea
           3. Statilia Messalina

A MAP OF THE ROMAN EMPIRE IN NERO'S TIME

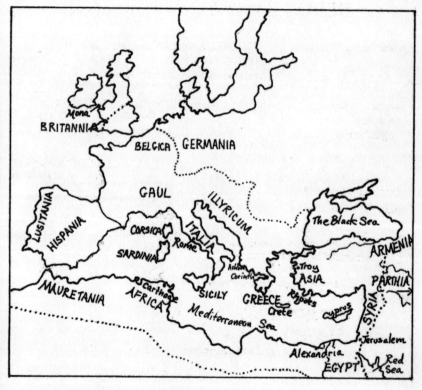

The dotted line shows the boundaries of the empire.

Lusitania = Portugal
Hispania = Spain

CHAPTER 1

The Emperor Sings

The most powerful man in the world was singing. A nod of his head was enough to make other heads roll; a tilt of his thumb was an order for throats to be cut; as soon as he wished it, grey-haired politicians would step into the bath and slit their wrists. But at this moment, in the theatre of Naples south of Rome, the Emperor, Nero Caesar* was moved to tears by the sound of his own voice.

It was 64 AD. The Roman Empire stretched as far as the borders of Parthia and Armenia. It included Upper

* All words marked with a star are explained in the Glossary at the back of the book

11

and Lower Germany, France, Spain, Portugal, Syria, Egypt and parts of Africa, as well as a chiunk of that bleak island in the North Sea which they called Britannia.

What Nero loved, though, was Art and Beauty. Expanses of conquered barbarian land were all very well, but an auditorium packed to bursting point with listeners was even better. This was as much of the world as he needed. He filled this space to its limits with his voice. The faceless people held their breath, enchanted, clearly, by his exquisite notes. And he enjoyed sweeping them away in the mighty wind of his emotions. While he sang, his fingers plucked busily at the strings of his tortoise-shell lyre.

The songs he sang were taken from the blackest moments in Greek tragedies, all packed with rape, murder, incest, lunacy, and savage revenge. There were no jokes to lighten the mood. Sweat flew off his ringlets and his grey eyes misted with grief as he threw himself into the sufferings of the heroes. When he roared the mad-scene from Hercules, he wore chains of solid gold round his ankles, and "rags" of tailored silk. Now he was Oedipus, who married his own mother by mistake and tore his eyes out with her brooch when he discovered the awful truth. Sometimes he put on a woman's mask – its mouth fixed in a shout of horror. Through it, he bellowed the complaints of Canace who saw her child thrown to the dogs. And with particular passion he threw himself into the role of Orestes, chased to the ends of the earth by the Furies*, because he had killed his own mother.

If anyone in the audience thought this in poor taste they kept it to themselves. Everyone was familiar with the graffiti on Roman walls:

Alcmaeon, Orestes and Nero are brothers.
Why? Because all of them murdered their mothers.

The recital had gone on for many hours. No one stirred. The whisper went round that a woman had given birth at the back of the auditorium, not daring either to leave or to utter a cry of pain. A few brave souls, in desperation, had dropped themselves down the back walls, nearly breaking their necks. Some, it was said, had pretended to die and been carried off in coffins.

The ground beneath Nero's feet trembled. His performance had clearly shaken the earth to its foundations. The rumbling mingled ominously with twanging strings. The Emperor's voice was nearly hoarse with strain and emotion. He loved that atmosphere, taut as a tent rope, when the world seemed to hang upon each little quiver of his throat.

Now the ground really was shaking. It might be just a tremor or it might turn out to be the beginnings of a full-scale earthquake. Still, although they might fear for their lives, no one moved. They didn't dare. Nero swept his hand across the strings in a final chord and a storm of applause broke forth, loud enough to make birds drop, stunned, out of the sky. How the people loved him! With grins of rapture on their faces they clapped as if their lives depended on it – which they did. But could they out-clap an earthquake?

Nero, with his usual regard for elegance and distinction, had ensured that the clapping would be of the highest quality. In that thundering roar something more refined and articulate could be heard. There were squadrons of well-paid young men placed about the audience: the "Bees", who made a loud humming noise; the "Roof-tiles", who clapped with hollowed hands; and the "Bricks", who clapped a dry staccato with flat hands. Each section had its own elaborate rhythms.

Those who didn't understand how it worked, or

where it came from, were thrilled by the exotic sound and joined in as best they could.

Nero had worked hard for this applause. In the earliest days of his reign he had summoned Terpnus the famous lyre-player to play to him for hours on end. And later, from Terpnus he took lessons. His fingertips blistered on the strings before they toughened up. To train his voice, he lay on the floor with slabs of lead on his chest. He swallowed disgusting potions to make himself vomit and keep his weight down. He gave up apples, nibbled dried figs and lived for days on chopped chives in olive oil. Even worse, he braved the disgust and disapproval of his mother – and the Senate, that august assembly of grand old men who liked to believe they still governed Rome. For a Roman aristocrat, let alone an Emperor, to perform publicly on stage was a disgrace. The old ruling classes had a severe, old-fashioned view of dignity, which Nero didn't share. So there he stood, unashamed, at the centre of the stage and of the world, encircled by a deafening roar of love, and rolling miles of fat Roman provinces.

After the show, when the Emperor had left and the people filed out, the earth quaked in earnest. The theatre collapsed in a heap of rubble, and some people whispered that the gods of the Infernal Regions* were offering a pointed comment. Nero saw it differently. He ordered praise and sacrifices to the immortal gods who had delayed the disaster till the show was over, thus preserving so many human lives. It was a mark of the highest favour that they had not permitted him, Nero, to be crushed in the middle of a song.

CHAPTER 2

The "Bronze-Beards"

The baby was born feet-first, which was usually considered a bad sign. But just as the midwife lifted him up, the first beam of morning light rounded the stone sill into the dark chamber, and lit up the infant in a pale gleam. Phoebus Apollo, lord of light and lyres, had marked him for his own. It was December 15th of the year 37AD, nine months after the death of the gloomy tyrant, Tiberius.

The summer palace at Antium was bleak at this time of year. The sea outside was grey and pounded angrily on the shore. Guests were arriving in carriages to congratulate the parents. The child's father, Ahenobarbus, received them with his customary snarl. Any child born to him and Agrippina, he declared, was sure to be a foul-natured beast and a public nuisance.

The child was a descendant, on both sides, of the first Emperor Augustus*, whose memory was revered because, 70 years before, he had brought peace to Rome after decades of bloody civil war. Augustus had taken over sole control of Rome and the provinces when he had defeated his colleague Mark Antony, and Cleopatra, queen of Egypt, in the famous sea battle at Actium off northwest Greece in 31BC.

The Summer Palace at Antium

For centuries Rome had been a Republic, governed by the Senate, a council of the city's most well born and distinguished men, as well as two Consuls elected by the Senate to hold joint power for one year at a time. The trouble was, though, that while the Romans believed passionately in the Republic as a way of governing, the system had ceased to be practical. Romans loved liberty, but they had become too quarrelsome, and there had been years of war and confusion.

It was out of this chaos that Augustus had emerged as the winner. What was needed in Rome was one strong man at the helm, whom no one dared to challenge. To keep the people happy, Augustus and the senators kept up all the appearances of a Republican government. Augustus modestly called himself the "First among equals", although there was no doubt who was really in charge and everyone knew the new regime was a thinly veiled monarchy. It was, in fact, the beginning of what we now call the Roman Empire, and Augustus was its first Emperor.

He controlled the Senate, and, when he died, he passed on his power to a new 'First among Equals', his stepson Tiberius. Under Tiberius's rule, scores of senators were executed in trumped-up treason trials.

There was grumbling no doubt, but senators were governed by fear. The biggest challenge now, if you belonged to the old ruling class, was just to stay alive.

The baby's mother, 23-year-old Agrippina, was the great-niece of the old Emperor Tiberius, and during his reign she had lost most of her family. Her father Germanicus was a war hero, adored by all Romans, and even Rome's enemies. People had suspected Tiberius of hating his nephew Germanicus, and when he'd died an untimely death in Syria, many people had called it foul play.

Germanicus' family was doomed, it seemed. After Germanicus's death, Agrippina's mother and two brothers had been exiled, beaten and starved to death by Tiberius. But now Tiberius himself was dead. It was hardly surprising that Agrippina had waited for the old tyrant to die before bringing a child of her own into the world. Luckily, she had one brother left, and now *he* was the new Emperor.

His name was Caligula, which means "Little-Boot". Years before, in the barracks in Germany, where his father had been such an admired general, the little boy had strutted up and down shouting commands in a pair of tiny soldiers' sandals. The tough old centurions had melted at the sight. It was a sweet name for one of the most mad and murderous monarchs ever to have ruled. In these early months of the reign he was still the people's darling, "chicken", "baby" and "pet", but the carnival would, soon enough, become a dance of death.

Egyptian kings used to marry their sisters and be worshipped as gods, and Caligula seemed to think these oriental habits a good idea. He loved all his sisters, particularly Drusilla. He fancied himself a god and his sisters "divine". When the old men of the Senate rose to speak, the first thing they said was: "Good Fortune attend the Emperor and his sisters." Indeed they said anything to please him. The Emperor was full of terrifying whims and caprices. If crossed, his love turned easily to hate.

One day, soon after Agrippina had given birth, Caligula came to see his new nephew. "What shall we call him?" Agrippina asked her brother. He peered at the wrinkly head, which lolled and drooled out of its woollen wrappers.

"Claudius?" he jested. The baby did have a passing resemblance to their uncle Claudius, a man who used to slobber unattractively from sadistic pleasure when watching the death agonies of gladiators, and wasted hours in his study on footling antiquarian research. The family was not proud of him and kept him out of sight. Agrippina didn't relish the joke. She was cast in the fine old Roman mould. Proud, clever, ambitious and beautiful, she had little patience with such imperfect specimens as her uncle Claudius.

She had been married off to a man named Ahenobarbus when she was thirteen. The surname Ahenobarbus means "Bronze-Beard". A distant ancestor in the earliest days of the Republic was said to have met the twin gods Castor and Pollux, who had stroked his cheek and turned his beard from black to bronze. Ever since then, a tawny beard and harsh arrogant temper had been the mark of the clan. "Who can wonder at the bronze beard?" said a famous orator, "when the nerves are of iron and the heart of lead?"

Agrippina's baby son was eventually given the name Lucius Domitius Ahenobarbus. He would be the last of the Bronze-Beards. The name Nero, by which he is known to history, came later.

CHAPTER 3

"A barber and a ballet dancer"...

When Nero was two, his aunt Drusilla, Caligula's favourite sister, died. From that moment on, laughing was declared a 'capital offence'. "What does that mean?" asked the boy. "It means look sad. If you laugh you die!" replied the nurse. Nero quickly rearranged his face into a frown, terrified lest a laugh or smile should escape him. The slaves found the sight of his droopy mouth dangerously comical.

Uncle Caligula fell out of love with his two remaining sisters. He accused them both of plotting against him – which was more than likely, though little is known of the details. He exiled Agrippina and her younger sister to some of those rocky little islands, which the Mediterranean Sea had spewed up expressly, it seemed, for the punishment of disgraced court ladies.

With his wife now languishing on a desert island, Ahenobarbus retired with his son to the countryside. In a convoy of rattling wagons they rumbled up those long paved roads that Romans were famous for, to the town of Pyrgi, on the coast north of Rome. Every day, Ahenobarbus swelled, as if rage were a pair of bellows blowing him up. He was dying of dropsy, a disease that makes the body bloat with water that it cannot get rid of. (A few pills can cure it now.)

Nero woke suddenly in the dark. "Come, your father is about to die," whispered his nurse. "You must call him by name and catch his last breath with your kiss. Only you are left to do it." This was a very ancient custom.

Nero did not like the smell of his father's breath – or his bristling hair and angry eyes. Wild boars' heads at banquets looked like that. With trembling fingers he tweaked at his father's eyelashes. The nurse said he had to shut the eyes, but they kept glaring and didn't want to shut. She had to help him a little. When, at last, it was done, some slave women came in with sponges and pots of water. Others set up a caterwauling noise like mountain jackals. The child ran back to his cot and pulled the covers over his head.

As the body crackled on the funeral pyre, Nero gazed at his ancestors. Their death masks, paraded on poles in the smokey sky, looked solemn and disapproving. Now his father was among them. He rubbed his stinging eyes and wondered where his mother was. He remembered her tinkling bracelets and her neck, which used to look like marble under its pallor of powdered lead and horn. When he kissed her the white powder used to come off on his lips and she had to dab them with a handkerchief.

Uncle Caligula now stole Nero's inheritance. Left

without money, and without a father or a mother, the boy was in need of protection, so Aunt Lepida, his father's sister, took him under her wing. "Poor penniless orphan!" she muttered, as she popped him into another of those wooden-wheeled wagons that shook the teeth out of your head. They headed south to Lepida's estates in Calabria – a good remote spot – to wait until Caligula's reign of terror was over.

Aunt Lepida left Nero to be cared for by her household slaves. "Reared by a barber and a ballet dancer," sneered the ancient historians of Nero's early life. That was just their way of emphasizing what they most disapproved of later on – his foppish curls and undignified antics on stage. In fact, any rich household might boast a barber and an entertainer among its slaves and it was normal for a Roman child to be surrounded by such people. There was plenty of fun to be had in a well-staffed house. Watching the barber at work was always diverting. All the men of the house came to him. Shaving was a perilous business in those days before stainless steel razors, and Nero watched eagerly as the barber's iron blade rasped across their bristly chins. If blood were drawn, the little boy would run to find cobwebs and vinegar for dressing the wound. (That's what they used for plasters in those days.)

The dancer was even more spellbinding. Nero would beat a rhythm with a spoon on a pot and watch him twirl round the colonnades, a one-man crowd of gods, heroes and monsters. How graceful he was! He never allowed a sound to pass his lips.

In this way Nero learnt his first Greek myths. Like all Roman children he learnt to speak Greek just as well as Latin, for many slaves were Greek. It was essential to be bilingual, as half the empire was Greek-speaking. Greece may have been a conquered land, but the great art, literature and philosophy of ancient Greece was revered by cultivated Romans even as they heaped abuse on their Greek slaves.

One day, when Nero was five, a messenger galloped into the yard. There were gasps of astonishment and excited discussions. Something had changed. Aunt Lepida bustled up to him, trying to look mournful but smiles kept breaking through. Taking the boy on her knee, she explained that members of his own Praetorian Guard had stabbed Uncle Caligula to death in the theatre.

"Such a shame! The young man started off so well. It's been a hard couple of years but now, thank the gods, we can head for Rome and see a bit of life again. I've had more than enough of the country. The new Emperor is your great-uncle Claudius and my very own son-in-law, my daughter Messalina's husband. When the trouble began, he hopped behind a curtain to hide. Who can blame him with all that mayhem going on? But a guardsman saw his toes, dragged him out and hailed him Emperor! To think... it never seemed like much of a match at the time, my pretty girl and that ugly old man. You, too, will be a happy boy. My son-in-law will allow your mother to come home."

CHAPTER 4

Life at court

Now Nero lived in a fine mansion in Rome. His mother had returned. Her fortune was restored, and she soon used her charm and beauty to steal a husband from her sister-in-law, Nero's aunt Domitia. Domitia was the elder sister of the Aunt Lepida who had taken care of Nero. The husband was a rich and inflential ex-Consul.

Divorce and remarriage were very common among the Romans. One woman was famous for marrying eleven times. In the great game of survival, husbands, wives, names, and even children, sometimes had to be reshuffled. Agrippina needed a strong man to protect her from the malice of her main rival in rank and beauty, the Empress Messalina – the wife of Agrippina's uncle Claudius, arguably the most powerful woman in the land, and much feared.

Now, of all the ill-fated children of the war hero Germanicus, only Agrippina was left. Her sister Livilla, not so well protected, had been banished again, and died soon after.) Agrippina was a survivor. celverness and beauty helped, but her trump card would always be her father the great Germanicus whom everyone loved. If he had lived to be Emperor he might have given people cause to love him less. But since he had died young, his memory was sanctified and Agrippina knew just how to make the most of his reflected glory.

When Nero was nine he performed in the "Troy Game", a ceremonial pageant, acted out on horseback by the sons of Roman nobles. The crowd loved young Nero's grey eyes, and golden hair, but most of all they wanted to roar their approval of the only grandchild of the tragic and noble Germanicus. For Britannicus, on the other hand, the son of Claudius and Messalina, they cheered less loudly. He was the Emperor's son – the one most likely to inherit the empire – but Nero had the right blood in his veins too and might one day become a serious rival.

The hatred between his mother and Messalina had been obvious to Nero from an early age. Messalina had once sent murderers to kill him when he lay sleeping in his crib. But a snake had slithered out from under his pillow and scared them away – so Agrippina said. She frightened Nero with this story and made him wear a snakeskin cased in gold as a bracelet on his arm. This would help him, she said, to remember who his enemies were.

But Messalina's days were numbered. She was Rome's bad girl – dangerous, lustful, spiteful and extravagant. "She's gone too far," Agrippina announced to her son one day when he was eleven.

"Imagine, poor benighted uncle Claudius, hobbling round Ostia with his plans for a fine light-house, while his wife back home throws an orgy and marries her lover in the middle of it all. And what did the blushing bride wear? A few scanty thongs of leopard skin. That's a party that will end in tears!"

The news of his wife's betrayal was broken to Claudius at Ostia, where he was engrossed in plans to create a new port for Rome. Crying and ranting in turn, he stormed back home.

"She made her last journey in a refuse cart," gloated Agrippina. "Her friends had vanished of course, and she wasn't let near her husband so she couldn't beg for her life. All your aunt Lepida could do was urge her daughter to kill herself before they caught her. But she botched it. I'm sure you'll never disgrace me in that way, my boy."

Nero shook his head vigorously.

"The tribune had to finish her off with his sword. What degradation!"

Within a year Claudius remarried. The new wife was Nero's mother Agrippina, his own niece. Her husband had died leaving her rich. Marriage between uncle and niece was considered incestuous, but as soon as the Senate understood the Emperor's desire, they changed the law. From now on it would be all right for men to marry their brothers' daughters. Uncles and nieces who wished to marry were urged to come forward at once, the more the merrier. Not many did.

On the day of the wedding, a young nobleman called Silanus cut his throat. The pointed timing of his suicide was the only luxury left to him. He had been betrothed since infancy to Octavia, Claudius's nine-year-old daughter. But Agrippina's secret longterm plan was that Octavia should instead eventually marry her own son Nero. To get rid of Silanus she had had him framed on – of all things – a charge of incest with his sister. Claudius had enjoyed nosing through the archives in search of ancient purification rites. To rid the city of the incest pollution caused by this "wicked young man", he sent priests to mumble dusty prayers in a sacred grove. This had caused much laughter at Roman dinner parties.

Octavia and her brother Britannicus were a gloomy pair. Barely a year had passed since their mother's death. Their last sight of her had been disturbing. She had been shivering with cold and fear – those tatty shreds of animal skin she wore might be fine party gear, but they weren't right for dying in. Even children could tell that. She had begged them to fall at their father's knees and plead for her life. But they couldn't get near his knees and they never saw her again. Her statues were removed, her name erased from inscriptions. Now they knew how completely a person could disappear. For weeks they had wept as they watched their father tuck into his evening banquet, cracking roast snails, chomping goose liver, beef and quinces, as if he'd never had a wife and they'd never had a mother.

But now they were to have a new mother. "Dearest

Octavia," purred Agrippina, "darling Britannicus, we are all family now. I will help your father in my small way with the burden he has to bear. I'm sure I admire him as much as you do. He is so replete with ancient wisdom, and so tender to his family. *You*, I know, will help *me*, and love your new brother, who has for so long been fatherless."

During the marriage ceremony it was hard for Claudius's children to keep the festive smile on their faces. They were lost in this palace of dark corridors. Their father had lost his grip and couldn't be counted on to look after them. This new wife squeezed him like a piece of warm wax.

As for Nero, he was excited by his move to the Palace. The very word palace comes from the Latin word *Palatium*, the name of the hill overlooking the Roman Forum,* where Tiberius had built the imperial residence. Nero had a taste for splendour. He also had a zest for fun and larks, which his mother's cold stares and the mournful incomprehension of his step-siblings failed to dampen. During the evening banquets – where the eunuch* Halotus, the imperial food-taster, was always on hand, checking every dish for poison – the imperial children would perch on their parents' couches.

Claudius liked to drink wine long into the night, and hold forth to his family.

"Have you heard, my dears, that a man has recently died because politeness prevented him from breaking wind when he needed to? When it comes to matters of health, as we see from this tragic example, Nature is supreme. We cannot trifle with her unshakeable rules."

With this he let out a finely tuned burp – to give nature her due. "I think I may put forward a motion in the senate to promote the cause of public wind-breaking, since a misplaced sense of decorum could imperil some of our most distinguished friends..."

Courtiers sat in respectful silence until he was carried off to bed. Sometimes, to ease his groaning stomach, he would order a slave to make him vomit by tickling his throat with a feather.

Agrippina moved fast to make her son the Golden Boy of Rome. First she arranged his betrothal to Claudius's daughter Octavia. The next step was even more significant. "The Emperor shows you the greatest honour, my dear; he will adopt you as his son. You are no longer Lucius Domitius of the house of Ahenobarbus. From now on you will be Nero Claudius Caesar Drusus Germanicus. Our friend Pallas has been hard at work on your behalf." Pallas was another of those detested Greek ex-slaves who ran the Empire behind the scenes. People whispered that he was Agrippina's lover. But this rumour had not reached Claudius's ears. He now dignified his wife with the title Augusta,* a name never granted, before, to any living Empress.

Nero's new name took him nearer to the top. And the top was where you had to get if you wanted to stay alive. Claudius had now made him the official heir to the empire. Britannicus called him by his old name one day, either out of spite or forgetfulness. Nero made sure his mother got to hear of it, and soon after, all Britannicus' tutors were executed. Claudius had done a terrible wrong to his own son.

The following year Nero was thirteen, and more honours were heaped on him. He was allowed, a whole year early, to put aside the purple-bordered toga of childhood, and wear instead the plain white "toga of manhood". He was graced with the title "Prince of Youth", as well as being a Consul* Elect, and honorary priest in four priestly brotherhoods.

For his tutor, and this was the greatest honour, Nero now had the most famous orator and philosopher of the

day, Lucius Annaeus Seneca. Seneca had narrowly escaped death years before on charges of adultery with Nero's aunt Livilla. Instead he had been exiled for nine years in Corsica, where his only entertainment had been writing letters to friends. "How trifling are mere worldly misfortunes," he had written, "to a mind that's nourished on stoic* philosophy!" Some of his other letters were less lofty: "Do whatever you can, pull every string, I beg you, to get me out of this hell hole! The mono-tony, these moronic grunting natives, this blistering wilderness where there is neither purpose nor conversation, are beyond endurance!"

Agrippina saved him. With a quick whisper in her husband's ear, she had him recalled and he was once again permitted to dazzle Rome with his verbal fireworks. She did not wish her son's mind to be clouded with philosophy, or any other kind of airy Greek nonsense, but the art of public speaking, rhetoric as it was called, was highly prized in Rome. When Nero was sixteen he made his first speeches in the Roman Forum, in both Latin and Greek.

Nero loved painting and sculpture; he wrote poetry; he took a delight in all things Greek. The fluid, subtle language suited his sensitive mind. His mother would have preferred him to have a more Roman temperament – resolute, robust, and practical. But apart from his passion for horses and chariot racing, his leanings were artistic. Modesty and mildness, above all, were the qualities urged upon him by his teacher. Seneca no doubt felt a heavy responsibility in the shaping of a prince who might rule the world. Anyone who had lived through the perilous reigns of Tiberius, Caligula and Claudius would have been the first to agree.

CHAPTER 5

"Mushrooms are the food of the gods"

In 54AD Agrippina was getting nervous. Her favourite informer had been expelled from the Senate. Claudius, drunk one night, had been heard to complain about his awful wives. And then one day he had hugged his forlorn son Britannicus. "I'll make it up to you my boy," he croaked, before shambling off.

A swarm of bees had settled on the Capitol and a pig was born with hawk's talons. Such freakish occurrences were taken very seriously as signs of change. Soothsayers and astrologers did good business. Agrippina decided it was time to seize power.

Before she acted, she had to make sure of her son's

heart and mind. His loyalty to her must be undivided. If he was to rule the world she must be sure of ruling him. She feared that her disapproving manner towards Nero might have been less seductive than his aunt Lepida's gossip and flattery. She summoned her son.

"Your aunt Lepida wishes me dead."

"What makes you think so?" replied Nero, anxiously.

" She has bound me with evil spells under the power of Hecate* and the fiends of the Underworld. Her slaves overheard her."

"I cannot believe it."

"Ah! You're taken in by her winning ways. But I have witnesses to prove it, and what's more, I already feel the effects of her black art. Don't be taken in by sweet looks. Of course, she wants you on her side. She fears you. And yes, she took you in when you were small. But whose grandmother is she?"

"Well of course she loves Britannicus too, but she and I have always been friends."

"It cannot be so any more. Here's what you will say at her trial..."

Sorcery and the cursing of enemies were a common activity among all classes of Romans. They wrote names on lead tablets, pierced them with nails and dunked

40

them in wells or springs. Toads' intestines, snake-bones and herbs from tombs were tossed into malignant cauldrons: "May burning fever seize all her limbs, kill her soul and her heart, *arourarelyoth*, let her body be twisted and shattered, *phrix phrox*..." This is just one example of the many curses archaeologists have dug up in England, Africa and Germany, as well as all over Italy.

It was easy to frame aunt Lepida. Quite apart from the charge of sorcery, which may or may not have been true, she had let her slaves run wild. They were threatening the peace of southern Italy. When he gave evidence at her trial, Nero dared not look at his aunt. His mother's steely glare was upon him. She dazzled him, playful and approachable one minute, fearsome and remote the next. Lepida was sentenced to death

And then it was Claudius's turn. It was October, the height of the mushroom season. Claudius loved mushrooms, and he met his death in a particularly succulent fungus that Halotus the food-taster had perched on top of the pile. Halotus, like many of Claudius's key servants, now took his instructions from Agrippina. Agrippin had acquired a deadly

paste from a notorious poisoner, called Locusta, and this had been smeared on the mushroom that Claudius ate. Claudius's own doctor then finished him off by tickling his throat with a poisonous feather.

The Emperor was already being wrapped in his funeral shroud when the news got about that he was feeling "a little unwell". The Palace gates were barred, and an order was sent out for sacrifices to be offered up for the Emperor's life. Britannicus and Octavia wanted to run and see their father, but Agrippina pounced on them and clasped them to her bosom.

"My dear Britannicus, you are the spitting image of your dear father!" she moaned. "How shall I endure it if he fails to recover?"

Agrippina did not want to announce his death until the lucky hour foretold by her astrologer. Until then she pretended her husband was still alive and kept a troupe of acrobats and clowns limbering up in the colonnades, "in case the emperor should rally and call for entertainment".

At last a slave came and whispered in her ear. She beat her breast and shouted, "Oh merciful gods, poor fatherless children! Our most August Emperor has paid his debt to Nature." Then she gripped her stepchildren tightly while the guards pushed open the massive doors to reveal a hushed crowd waiting outside. The seventeen-year-old Nero stepped out into the golden light of an October morning. At his side was Burrus, commander of the Praetorian Guard, who owed his promotion to Agrippina. No one could rule Rome without the support of his crack regiment of unshakeably loyal bodyguards. An officer stepped forward and hailed Nero Emperor. Nero looked about him with a beating heart. Some people might have expected Britannicus to be the new Emperor. But would anyone dare to utter his name? If they did, they got no answer. Nero heard behind him the thud of the Palace door being bolted again. Britannicus, half suffocating in his stepmother's perfumed arms, knew his fate was sealed.

"The password Sir?" (It was a tradition that everyday the Emperor gave out a new password to his palace guards.)

Nero faced the crowd. Though he had faith in Burrus he felt a little shocked that his mother was on the other side of the door. She had put everything into place, but was now invisible. The world's gaze was upon him alone. After a short hesitation, people were beginning to cheer. A guardsman was leaning intently towards him.

"The password?"

"Optima Mater" murmured the new Emperor. This is the Latin for "best of mothers".

Nero heard it repeated down the line. Like an echo being drummed into his own mind. A child's lesson in gratitude. He was pulled into a litter and borne over the heads of the crowd.

CHAPTER 6

Power

Now Nero was an Emperor, and Claudius also enjoyed a promotion – being dead, he was pronounced a god. Agrippina wanted to manage them both.

Claudius was easy to manage, not being able to speak up for himself. It was the final joke in a life of absurdities, that this unappetising member of the human race, whose treason-trials and executions had wrought havoc among the senatorial class, and whose exit by food-poisoning had been distinctly squalid, should now be deified. Better still, that the chief priestess of his new cult should be the woman whom everyone believed to have murdered him. Without a hint of a smile Agrippina studied designs for the Temple of the new god Claudius which was to be built on the edge of the Caelian hill. Nero lacked gravity and could not resist a joke: "mushrooms are the food of the gods", he would say, whenever he saw a platful.

All over the Empire, managers of imperial mints (the Empire's money-making factories) breathed sighs of relief. They had been juggling the heads of Nero and Britannicus on their coins, uncertain which to plump for. Their cities might be penalised if they made the wrong choice. Now it was simple. On one coin, the twin heads of Nero and his mother appeared face to face on the "heads" side. On another coin, Agrippina took up the whole of the "heads" side and Nero occupied the "tails" side. From Egypt to Colchester, everyone would understand, from this, who was really in charge.

But, though Agrippina's power could be blazed forth in shiny metal to the far-flung outposts of the Empire, in Rome she still had to hide behind a curtain when listening to debates in the Senate. One day, when Nero was receiving envoys from Armenia, she entered the council chamber wearing cloth of gold and crackling with gems. She headed for the platform to sit beside her son.

Seneca and Burrus made secret signals to Nero. A

woman could not sit on the imperial platform. That would be going too far. With a great show of courtesy Nero rose to greet her. The meeting could be resumed later, he said, as he escorted her from the room.

Modesty, Justice and Clemency. These were to be the keynotes of the new reign. There was hope in the air, just as there had been at the beginning of Caligula's reign, but it was more subdued. Romans had learnt that, although old men might be grumpy and vicious, young men could be worse. Especially young men with mothers like Agrippina. For she was of the killing sort.

Seneca was chief adviser in Nero's "Council of the Emperor's friends": "You must understand," he said to Nero, "that Senators will not submit to being ruled by a woman."

"Who says that they are? They are not even ruled by me. You wrote the speech yourself in which I restored their old powers. What more do they want?"

"Your mother has been heard to boast of her power over you. It doesn't help at all if you ride through the Forum with her, in a covered litter*, and then climb out with a crumpled toga."

"You mean that rides in a litter with my own mother are improper?"

"I hope you'll excuse my mentioning it but Romans are gossipy. People wonder what's going on behind the curtains. If you left them un-drawn there'd be fewer comments on the subject."

"What are you trying to say?"

"Only that your mother is still a beautiful woman, and permits you to kiss her like a lover, in public."

"Just our little joke. I get carried away when she's in a good mood with me – it's rare enough."

"Your high spirits must delight her, but your "little joke" is fodder for malicious tongues. Of course, in all other respects, your approachability and friendly manners will do wonders. The way you remembered the names of those Knights in the Forum yesterday was admirable."

"I'm glad you noticed that."

"Yes, remembering the names of unimportant people is the best way to show your desire to please. Which is particularly important just now, since the sudden death of our governor in Asia has made a very poor impression. Everyone fears the bad old ways. Poisonous banquets are not the thing any more. Wouldn't you agree?"

"Absolutely. That death was regrettable. I told my

mother she must not take such steps again without consulting me."

Silanus, the governor of Asia, had been such an inoffensive man that people called him "the golden sheep". He was the first casualty of the new reign. It was his brother who had cut his throat on the day of Agrippina's marriage to Claudius. Theirs was a blighted family, for they were great grandsons of Augustus, and therefore as nobly born as Nero himself. And Nero feared anyone whose blood gave them as good a claim to power as he had. Even so, he had not ordered this death. It was Agrippina who had been too busy on his behalf. For all her cunning, his mother could turn out to be more a liability than a help. At this point in his reign, after all, Nero wished to inspire confidence and optimism, not fear.

***

In December the air was filled with wood-smoke and the meaty smell of roasting bullocks. They swung round on spits, dedicated to Saturn, the god who had taught men to sow crops. It was the festival called "*Saturnalia*". Children with rag-bound feet shuffled into the firelight, grabbing at half-eaten joints. And Nero and his companions lurched through the "Field of Mars"* in floppy festive hats, soused in wine.

No one recognised the Emperor for in the days before photographs, it was easier for a famous person to go about incognito. Old crones plucked at his sleeve and scolded him for his rudeness. Young women slapped his face when he kissed them. Little boys beat him off, clawing and scratching when he tried to squeeze them.

The Emperor and his friends loped through the vegetable-market by the river Tiber, pelting each other with nuts and old cabbage leaves. Further on, by the warehouses on the riverbank they broke into a wine-merchant's depot and cracked a pot over the head of a barking dog. They squelched through the cattle market and, when Nero's friend Otho tripped over a step by the Great Altar of Hercules, Nero called him a clumsy buffalo. They mooed with laughter. As they reached the Palatine*, slaves scurried about lighting candles, preparing a feast. In some households, the Saturnalia was a holiday for slaves, but not here in the Palace.

Nero was "King of Fun" that night, which meant thinking up silly forfeits for his friends to perform. Nothing too demanding. Reciting a line of the *Iliad** backwards, spitting olive pips into a pot, knocking over pyramids of nuts... everything was wildly funny. And now it was the turn of Nero's stepbrother, young Britannicus.

"Tweet little bird, wag your beak, it's song time," cajoled Nero. The boy found himself lifted on to the table among the dishes heaped with flesh and fruit. His legs looked frail next to those fat haunches of venison. He didn't try to be amusing. A hush fell upon the room as he sang, in a tremulous fluting voice, about a prince, disinherited and reduced to slavery in his own house. It was a lament in which there was neither hope nor fear, only bitter resignation. Nero was vexed by the dampening effect it had upon his friends. They were touched with pity for the child. How long could he hope to live?

The *Saturnalia* is a Feast of Fools, and serious matters could be made light of. Even gods could be mocked. On one of these winter evenings the court gathered to watch a comedy called "*The Pumpkin-ification of Claudius*". It was a skit written by Seneca, Nero's tutor, on the death and deification* of the recent emperor. Fragments of it still survive.

The humour was extremely crude, and you would scarcely have believed that its author was the same man

who wrote such enlightened passages elsewhere about virtue and the shared humanity of men. That said, Seneca did have Claudius to thank for his nine dismal years in exile in Corsica. No doubt, after a few goblets of Falernian wine, the show had everyone in stitches. But it's hard to imagine Agrippina, chief priestess of the cult, or either of the new god's children, rolling in the aisles.

When Agrippina summoned Nero early in the new year, it was clear that the festive season was over.

"Are you so unsuited to the dignity of your office? How long did you think it would be before I got to hear of it?"

"What are we talking about, mother?"

"Your Greekling slut of a girl-friend is what we're talking about! Just show me this Acte, this ex-slave that Nero has taken to his bosom... and the flunkeys who are prepared to swear she's of royal stock – the "Attalids of

Pergamum" indeed! Who cooked up *that* little family tree?"

"I imagine her family pedigree is the least of your worries, mother,"

"I gave you Octavia for a wife! The Empire, no less, was her dowry. But whatever I put in place, you must undo, I suppose. My daughter-in-law the maidservant, eh! How openly you scorn *my* efforts and *your* obligations!"

"Well... not *openly* mother."

"No. You, who rule the world, were creeping about like a thief in the night. Helped by that ungrateful pair of pimps, the ex-convict and that cripple, Burrus. They forget my favours. And as for. you, it's clear that now the ship's in safe harbour, the captain who steered it there counts for nothing."

"Don't think I've forgotten what you've done for me, mother."

"You think I've served my purpose and cannot undo what I've done. The fact is you're overboard, yes, *drowning* in the flattery of friends and the arms of a slave. Why do you think Burrus and Seneca have helped along your little love affair? "

"You're enraged, mother. What can I say?"

"They're only too happy to soften your brains with love, while they get on with the business of government. Sometimes I begin to wonder if I've backed the wrong boy! Don't trifle with the daughter of Germanicus! The Praetorians are mine, heart and soul!"

"What will you do with them mother? Run to the barracks and shout 'Hail Britannicus'? Do so. I'll retire to Rhodes and take Acte with me."

Now that he'd said it, he loved the idea. Beside a blue sea, Acte would nestle on his lap and listen, spellbound, to his songs on the lyre. He would paint and sculpt and wrestle like a Greek athlete. Who was better suited than he to a life of private leisure? Acte adored him with gratitude and humility. She made him feel proud, and never nagged. The truth was that Nero felt at ease with self-made men and ex-slaves, people who didn't fret about insults to their dignity. How dull his wife Octavia was, with her noble ancestry. A mere child, besides, as sour as a green grape...

His fantasy of an idyllic life with Acte in Rhodes was dampened by just one sobering thought: there had been live emperors, and dead emperors, but never any *retired* emperors.

Britannicus died in February, just before his fourteenth birthday. There was a shocked silence at the children's table as the boy pitched off his couch gasping for breath.

"Not to worry," Nero reassured his dinner-guests laughing, "he's had these epileptic fits since childhood. He'll be fine tomorrow." The Emperor continued eating and drinking while his stepbrother was carried from the hall. Britannicus was buried the same night in the mausoleum* of Augustus on the Field of Mars.* Only screech owls and slaves attended the funeral. The slaves, it was said, had painted the corpse with gypsum to hide the discoloured flesh, but icy rain washed it away.

Perhaps Britannicus *did* die of epilepsy, a disease which can cause a darkening of the corpse. But it would have been a strange quirk of fate if he had died accidentally, when he was so clearly destined to be murdered. The pathos of his singing at the *Saturnalia* had enraged Nero, who also feared that Agrippina might, in a rage, take up his cause if she felt too disappointed by her own son. It was said that the preparations for Britannicus' hasty funeral had been made even before the boy began to feel unwell. The dismay in Agrippina's face, which she couldn't manage to conceal, was remembered long afterwards. A death in the palace which *she* hadn't ordered was a frightening novelty. Octavia, on the other hand, revealed no emotion.

CHAPTER 7

"The sullen tiger pads his gilded stage"

On the empire's new-minted coins, a change was noticed. Agrippina's face, like an eclipsed star, now peeped out from *behind* her son's. She was moved out of the palace to a mansion nearby, and her bodyguard dismissed. Her faithful crony Pallas, the "minister for finance", was also dismissed from his job. When Nero came to call on her, his greetings were cold and formal.

Old enemies, of whom Agrippina had plenty, smelt blood; and, determined not to miss the opportunity, sent Paris, Nero's favourite dancer, to break the news of a plot against him by his own mother.

Nero's heart began to pound. His own mother turning on him? His worst fears seemed to be realized. His eyes bulged. He sweated and gulped for breath. He sent for Seneca and Burrus, even though it was the middle of the night.

"Let's not get carried away," urged Seneca.

"Anyone has the right to a defence. A mother, most of all," said Burrus. "We'll go to her at daybreak with witnesses and see what she has to say."

Burrus was a decent man, loyal to Nero, but mindful of his obligations to the woman who had placed him at the head of the Praetorian Guard. He was stolid and practical. Seneca, on the other hand, had a brilliant mind and a way with words. They made a good partnership. They respected each other. Between the two of them, they hoped the young Emperor's excesses might be trimmed, and his life steered along safe lines.

The plot against Agrippina failed. She beat off her enemies with a spirited denial. "What kind of mother do they think I am? That shameless trollop, Silana – she has never had children. She thinks they can be exchanged as readily as lovers. She hates me because I advised young Africanus not to marry her, the old hag! And as for that Domitia," (this was her elder sister-in-law, whose husband Agrippina had stolen years before), "it's clear she had a few scores to settle."

But Agrippina did not recover her former supremacy. She retired to her seaside villa at Antium, and Nero, breathing more freely in her absence, got on with the daily business of being Emperor. He had to sit as judge in the law court. During the night, he read the written opinions of his advisers, and then delivered his verdict next morning. Being young and inexperienced, he took great trouble over it.

These were years of good government. Looking back on them later, the Emperor Trajan said they were the best five years in the history of the Empire. The informers, who had earned great rewards by setting up treason-trials in the previous reign, were suppressed. Corrupt governors of provinces, particularly in rich Asia, were called to account for greed and extravagance. Public order was tightened; provisions were made against forgery. The Senate was treated as if it still mattered.

Above all, an Emperor's job was to provide what the people cared about most: "bread and circuses", as the poet Juvenal scornfully put it. In Nero's time, one fifth of Rome's population depended on free handouts of corn. If the fleets of grain ships coming from Alexandria and Sicily were wrecked, people would starve. Sometimes ugly rumours caused rioting. And there were often shortages because the nearest harbour to Rome was Puteoli, just north of the Bay of Naples, and it was difficult to transport the grain from there to the huge granaries in Rome itself. To get up the shallow Tiber*, cargoes had to be transferred from the large ships on to lighter barges which were easily wrecked by high winds as they went up the coast.

Years earlier, Claudius had set about the task of turning Ostia, at the mouth of the Tiber*, into a decent harbour – not an easy task because of the silt washed down by the river as it ran out into the sea. He had died befor e he could complete it, butnow, no one paid more attention to the problem of Rome's corn supply than Nero.

He finished Claudius's engineering works at Ostia, abolished property tax on merchant shipping, and in 57AD gave out sums of 400 sesterces a head to the poor of Rome. He also opened a huge new market building on the Caelian hill near the Temple of Claudius. This made him popular with the common people. The senators were another matter.

Another area in which Nero took a particular personal interest was the gladatorial games. He disliked the spectacle of slaves being butchered in the arena. His tutor, Seneca, had been one of the first Romans to deplore the cruelty and the brutalising effect of the games on the public. The famous building we now call the Colosseum was built by later Emperors. But Nero *did* build Rome's first permanent wooden amphitheatre in the Field of Mars. And he did his best to to transform the bloody entertainment into something elegant, witty and magical. There would be fencing matches with celebrity guest stars or novelties, such as dwarves, or women-fighters. He decreed that no one should die at the end of the fight, not even the condemned criminals who made up the bulk of gladiators. When, eventually, the rabble's thirst for blood proved irresistible, he allowed that the gladiators should die but ordered that their coffins should be studded with amber.

Nero loved ingenious contraptions. The floor of the arena might suddenly roll apart to reveal scented saffron fountains, and thickets full of snarling animals. Beast-fighters darted nimbly among them. It was hard in this forest of teeth and tusks not to end up as tiger meat. Huge numbers of exotic creatures: gnu, wart hogs, giraffes, hippopotami, tigers, lions and elephants were hunted in Africa and shipped over. The poet Petronius wrote about it:

> Hunters, hawkers of death. And the market for murder
> > at Rome:
> Fangs in demand. At sea sheer hunger prowls the ships;
> On silken feet the sullen tiger pads his gilded stage,
> Crouches at Rome, and leaps! And the man gored
> > and dying,
> While the crowd goes wild.

The arena could even be flooded for the staging of sea-battles between "Greeks" and "Persians". There were spectacular displays of "sea monsters". There was an Arctic scene with polar bears and seals. An elephant, with a Knight on its back, performed a miraculous tightrope-walk. One day the cavalry of the Praetorian Guard took on four hundred boars and three hundred lions. To keep the spectators safe, nets were draped from elephant tusks; and rolling cylinders, like treadmills, were placed round the edge of the arena to prevent animals from leaping out.

One of Nero's duties was to perform sacrifices before the steps of Rome's huge temples. The scented smoke from the tripod, and the mesmerizing flute, made it easier to be solemn. Before assembled dignitaries and grim Vestal Virgins, he would sprinkle the *mola salsa*, a holy powder of salt and grain, between the horns of the sacrificial beast, then turn towards the sanctum of the god, and chant the same prayers that his ancestors had chanted, since time began. When he had finished, the *Popa* would whack the animal on the head to stun it, and the *Cultrarius*, (the "Knife-man") would slit its throat. If Nero scrambled the words, or the animal tried to run away, or the blood didn't flow freely, or the liver didn't look good, he would have to do it again, with extras the second time round.

After a day of such solemnities, parched with smoke and sickened by blood, Nero sometimes felt the need to run wild. He and his friends whooped through slums and taverns like a bunch of hoodlums, in wigs and baggy cloaks, assaulting whomever they met on the streets. One night, they started a fight with a Senator called Montanus. He hit back, but then began to apologize; a fatal mistake, since Nero, fearing he'd been recognized, obliged him to commit suicide. After that, a retinue of guards followed the young men at a discreet distance to make sure no resistance was offered.

Nero's every whim could be satisfied. When it came to sex, he had a great many whims, sometimes of a very experimental nature. He wanted to break all bounds, and to prove that everyone else was as lustful and uncontrolled as he was, if they would but admit it. To anyone who confessed to a little depravity, Nero was charm itself.

Tacitus and Suetonius, two disapproving Roman historians, writing a generation later, reported some sensational parties, Senators' wives floating over lakes on rafts in skimpy costumes, and ecstatic raves in wild-beast skins. Like many Romans Nero was openly bisexual and enjoyed some very public romps with beautiful young men.

Romans went wild over the acrobatic ballet dancers or "*pantomimes*", as they were called. The Greek word *pantomime* meant something very different then – not a Christmas show, but simply, *"a person who imitates everything"*.

Dressed in silky robes with tight-fitting masks, performers would mime myths or scenes from tragedies, to the musical accompaniment of a choir and an orchestra of flutes, drums, lyres and trumpets. Seneca's nephew Lucan wrote fourteen librettos for these choirs. They sang like chanting monks, but with a slightly Eastern sound that would remind a modern listener of Greek or Indian music. The ballet dancers skipped adroitly from one role to another, and spoke so cleverly with their hands that a prince from one of Nero's distant dominions begged the Emperor to send him a *pantomime* to help him communicate with foreign envoys. There would be no need for translators; instead of a babble of foreign tongues, there would be a beautiful silence as the dancer made everything clear with his graceful gestures.

Ballet was so much the rage that even an 80-year-old lady took to the dance-floor. And Nero himself took dancing lessons from his favourite dancer, Paris, the freedman* of his aunt Domitia. He hoped one day to graduate to the star role of Turnus, the young hero in Virgil's *Aeneid*. But he didn't shine. Though handsome, with fair curls and grey eyes, his legs were thin, his neck too thick, and his belly jutted out.

Instead, Nero dedicated himself to another art, that of the tragic actor. Actors at that time resembled the star singers of modern day musicals. The famous Greek tragedies of Euripides and Sophocles had been simplified into musical shows in which nearly every word was sung, not spoken. Actors composed and sang their own songs while accompanying themselves on the lyre. This was to become Nero's ruling passion. It was at this time that he became a pupil of Terpnus, the greatest lyre player of his time. Nero had a husky bass voice that lent itself to desperate and shocking roles. He too wrote his own songs. At dinner parties with literary friends, he would introduce a subject and his guests would improvise verses and round off each other's couplets with their own triumphant rhymes long into the night.

But Nero knew how much Agrippina disapproved of his "effeminate Greek hobbies". Sometimes her withering comments were reported back to him, spiced up by enemies. She was only forty-three and still beautiful. She could still marry a descendant of Augustus and turn the tables on him....

CHAPTER 8

"Best of Mothers..."

It was the festival of Minerva*, late March 59 AD. Merry voices rang out from Nero's villa in the fashionable seaside resort of Baiae. The Emperor was particularly genial. He had invited his mother to a feast and set her at the couch of honour. He went out of his way to flatter and delight her with some serious talk about the very thing that bored him: politics. "No doubt you heard, mother, about my plan last year to abolish indirect taxation. I'm still convinced it would have livened up trade... it takes a man of vision to think up these things, but the Senate, as usual, put a damper on it..."

Agrippina was entranced by the change in him. But

cunning and cautious as ever, she behaved as if nothing could interest her less than affairs of state. She could hardly be dragged away from the subject of homes and gardens. Return to Rome? Meddle in politics again? Those were the last things on her mind!

"That bronze Apollo I ordered from Corinth was a masterpiece." she purred. "The colonnade will extend as far as the fishponds, with twelve pillars on each side, of peach-blossom marble... the carp are stupendous this year, you should come and see them..."

Nero was amused to hear his haughty mother talk even of ballet dancers – as if she could fool him: "I was horrified to hear of your near-miss at the theatre, dear boy... I've always thought those mime artistes were dangerous enough without dropping out of the sky on to people's heads."

"Ah, you heard about that?" Nero had been badly frightened one night when a pantomime had dropped off his trapeze, hurtled past his right ear and crashed to the floor at his feet. "Yes, I had the stage technicians flogged, but no-one's been eager to use the flying equipment any more since then. Poor Icarus! He landed so close, I was splashed with his blood, mother."

It was a calm starlit night. The slaves' torches lit up

the landing stage as Nero escorted his mother to the imperial galley.

"A perfect night for boating, mother. Think of me bumping along the road as you glide over the bay..."

He laid his head on the silk stole that fell in soft pleats round her throat. With playful gallantry he kissed first one breast and then the other...

As the boat glided out on the water, Agrippina lay in the cabin on plumped cushions, with her companion Acerronia Polla curled up at her feet. "Aren't you pleased, my lady? What a warm reconciliation after all these frosty months! He's yours again..."

Agrippina looked thoughtful and said nothing. The galley's creaking timbers and the plash of its oars had a soothing rhythm.

Suddenly, the creaking turned into a squeal of splintering wood. But there was no time to think or wonder why before several tons of lead shot through the cabin roof with deadly speed. Agrippina's escort, Gallus, was crushed and killed instantly, but the side beams of Agrippina's couch just held the weight of the collapsing boat off their heads. The sea began to gush through the scuppered planks and the galley pitched over to one side.

It was a scene of almost comical confusion as half of

the crew appeared to be trying hard to sink the vessel, while others, who weren't in on the plot, tried to save it. But as it tilted, Agrippina and Acerronia rolled out through a narrow space into the sea. Acerronia was not much of a swimmer. She thrashed about in the icy water shouting, "Save me – I'm the Emperor's mother!" Perhaps she had hoped to be rescued first, by pretending to be her mistress. If so, it was a bad idea, as the sailors hacked her to pieces with oars and boat hooks. As the mangled body floated off into the night, Agrippina swam very quietly in the opposite direction, towards the shore. Some astonished fishermen pulled her out of the water into their boat, and took her to her villa by the Lucrine Lake.

Wounded and shivering, she realized that her only

hope lay in pretending not to understand that Nero had planned her death. Crowds of loyal well-wishers gathered round her villa. But inside, her own slaves began to understand the situation, and, one by one, they slipped away. She sent her freedman Agerinus to Nero to say that she had survived an accident, but he shouldn't come to her yet, as she was too exhausted by the long cold swim.

Nero was in a pitiful state of nerves when Agerinus arrived. The plan had been a shambles. He knew his mother would not believe it had been an accident. Her reproachful face haunted him in the dark like a gorgon. She might, even now, be gathering an army together. The only solution was to pretend that *she* had tried to kill *him*. It was clumsy and undignified but it had to be done. He threw a sword to the floor at Agerinus' feet and shouted "assassin!"

Some Guardsmen clapped the bewildered messenger in chains and led him away. Nero sent for Seneca and Burrus, who were fast asleep, and put them in the picture. They were horrified. "A shipwreck on a calm night like this? Who dreamt up such an idiotic plan?"

Nero pointed to Anicetus, one of his old tutors, now commander of the fleet at Misenum. It had been a delicate matter inviting someone to murder his mother – not a subject he had wished to broach with his more distinguished advisers. Now they had to make the best of a bad job.

"Clearly she has to die tonight, one way or another, but you won't get my Praetorians to kill a daughter of Germanicus," said Burrus. "I'll take some armed marines," replied Anicetus. "If we don't hurry we could have a civil war by the morning."

Agrippina lay alone in a dark room. Her shoulder had been gashed as she rolled off the boat. Now it throbbed painfully. In the first few hours after her return, the slaves had still answered her call. While some of them were binding the wound she had ordered others to open up Acerronia's will. She never tired of money and was eager to see what the woman had left her. The present pain and anxiety might be dispelled a little by the pleasure of new possessions – she could pretend to herself that she still had a long life ahead in which to enjoy them.

But now since the slaves had melted away and failed to light the lamps properly before they left, she felt weary. Acerronia had been a fool to die like that. Possibly she had smelt a rat and shouted out as a decoy to help her mistress escape. A fool either way. It was silent inside the villa, but outside, there was a hum of voices where the villagers were waiting for news. And then a sudden hush fell upon the crowd. Marching feet could be heard outside the villa.

Could it be Nero and his bodyguard rushing to comfort his mother for her unpleasant adventure? Agrippina seized on this thought. They could be heard now in the courtyard, these brisk, tramping feet – no sound of a human voice. There was no slave to announce them – nor anyone to stop them. The men who burst so abruptly through the door and loomed over her bed were clearly not there to inquire after her health. She didn't bother to stand up. "You do not come at my son's orders," she said to them. They didn't reply. These grim faced men were not Praetorians, and didn't in the least care who her father was. One of them struck her hard on the head. She gasped, "strike here" – pointing to her womb: "strike here, at the body that nurtured Nero!"

CHAPTER 9

"Miss Domitia Nero"

Seneca drafted a letter to the Senate. It denounced Agrippina for plotting against her son; and listed her crimes, committed when she was the wife of Claudius. Her birthday was declared a day of ill omen and Nero nursed his shattered nerves for six months in Naples before returning to Rome in September. The Best of Mothers, to whom he owed so much, no longer belittled him with her withering comments. At last he could allow his artistic side to bloom.

Romans didn't like the idea of a man killing his own mother, although they could still manage to make jokes about it. But singing and playing the lyre in public was going a step too far. Burrus and Seneca did their best to talk Nero out of making his debut in a public theatre. "Why waste good music on the man in the street?" they urged. "You've a very fine private theatre on the Vatican hill. It would be a splendid party, a select circle of close friends..."

"Singing is sacred to Apollo." he beamed at them. "That glorious and provident god is represented in a musician's dress in Greek cities, and in Roman temples as well..."

And now, "like a Greek pansy", sneered Senators among friends, "or a Saturnalian call girl, he performs in a flower-patterned tunic without belt or shoes, and bright silk scarves about his neck..."

The Greens were Nero's favourite team of charioteers, and so he had the track of the *Circus Maximus*, (the great race course) strewn with green copper dust. Now he wanted to be a charioteer and practised hard, drinking a potion of dried boar's dung in water, which, according to Roman doctors, fortified the body against sporting injuries.

"This must be kept private," said Burrus and Seneca with stern emphasis. "An Emperor careering round the *Circus Maximus* really wouldn't do. Might we suggest that you finish work on that private race course in the Vatican Fields and inaugurate it with a small gathering?"

"Chariot racing," Nero pulled himself up haughtily, "was an accomplishment of ancient kings. It has been honoured by poets – and sculptors. Look at any temple roof and what do you see? Gods riding about in chariots."

Nero wanted to share his love of art, music, poetry and Greek athletics with his people. He wanted to encourage the higher orders to overcome their stuffy prejudices and play and sing in public like him. Though of course none of them must play or sing *better* than him. Those who had a talent for clapping came top on his list of favourites.

In the year of his mother's death, he created "The Youth Games". In the lives of all Roman youths there was an important family ceremony when they shaved their first beards. The time had now come for the twenty-two-year old Emperor to perform his ritual "first shave". He placed the trimmings in a pearl casket and dedicated them, with great pomp, and the sacrifice of hundreds of bullocks, to Jupiter on the Capitol*. The climax of the festival was Nero's recital in a private theatre, with other handpicked, performing aristocrats. The song he chose for this occasion was "The delirium of the Bacchants". According to myth, the Bacchants were frenzied women who followed the cult of Bacchus, god of wine, and under his influence, tore the young king of Thebes into tiny slivers. Such a theme offered great scope for expressive singing. The old soldier Burrus was there with a whole battalion, struggling to keep a cheerful expression. He clapped till his hands stung.

The following year, Nero set up more games: *"The Neronia"* to celebrate October 13th, the anniversary of his becoming Emperor. There would be competitions of music, poetry and public speaking; athletics, gymnastics, and chariot racing. He built a magnificent gymnasium in the Field of Mars, next to his newly built public baths, where Romans from the lowest to the highest could wallow on slabs of polished marble, or strut over dazzling mosaics of dolphins and sea nymphs. Nero himself could be seen there in a loincloth, singing as he performed his exercises. Perhaps he might even wrestle in the next Olympics...

In fact, wrestling was the only form of combat Nero ever engaged in. Augustus and Tiberius had been soldier Emperors. Even limping Claudius had toured Britain in a chariot and celebrated a triumph for his invasion of that turbulent island – hence the name of his unlucky son Britannicus. Now there was trouble again at this northern frontier of the empire, but Nero was not tempted to go there in person or take part in any fighting himself.

In 59 AD he sent a new commander to Britain called Gaius Suetonius Paulinus, to storm Mona (now Anglesey in North Wales). The Druids, sworn enemies of Rome, had made the island into a stronghold from which they fostered rebellion, even across the sea in Gaul. These warrior-priests were dedicated to the savage old Celtic gods. They took prisoners only so that they could kill them later, with hideous ceremonies on the altars in their sacred groves.

In order to attack Mona, the Romans had to cross the stretch of water, which separated the island from the shore of north Wales – the Menai Strait. Waiting for a low tide, the cavalry swam with their horses and the infantry rowed in flat-bottomed boats. The sight of their enemies lined up on the beach was enough to make the bravest heart quail. Not only the Druids themselves but also their women stood ready to fight – such women as Romans had never seen, witches in black cloaks with long hair spraying in the wind. Smoke and flames leapt from their torches and they screamed deadly curses. If looks could kill they should have won. In fact, if the Romans had been on their feet they might well have run for their lives, but it's hard for a swimming army to turn around. In the end, the Romans overcame their panic, clambered up the shore, and burnt the snarling Druids with their own fire.

Their triumph was brief. In 61 AD a new rebel emerged on the other side of Britain: Queen Boudicca of the Iceni tribe in East Anglia. She was a commanding personality, harsh-voiced and tall, and "more intelligent than most women are," as Tacitus, the Roman historian, grudgingly admits. The reports that had reached her from Rome of Nero's artistic leanings had led her to believe she was twice the man he was. She called the Emperor of Rome "*Miss* Domitia Nero", and led a savage revolt against Britain's Roman rulers with the help of the Trinobantes of Essex, massacring first the garrison in *Camulodunum* (Colchester), then the river port of *Londinium*, (London), and finally *Verulamium* (St Albans). Boudicca's army slaughtered 70,000 Romans and Romanised Britons. She hoped for support from Queen Cartimandua in the North. But this was the

queen who had betrayed the British freedom fighter
Caratacus to the Romans ten years before in 51 AD.

Cartimandua refused to help and Boudicca was
defeated finally at Atherstone in Warwickshire.
Conquered enemies could expect to be paraded in triumph through the streets of Rome. And that was not the
worst of it. At the very moment that the victorious

general offered the spoils of war to Jupiter, his captives would be garrotted in a foul-smelling pit at the base of the Capitol. But sometimes emperors were eager to show their clemency. Claudius had spared Caratacus. Nero might also have shown mercy, but Boudicca didn't give him the chance. She took poison, and so he never got to see her famous tunic of many colours or the thick blonde hair that swished round her hips.

Nero's lack of enthusiasm for war or conquest made him unpopular with the old ruling classes. But it was good for his humbler subjects, and saved both lives and money. He now had to decide whether to punish Britain and its conquered tribes, or adopt a milder, more constructive policy. He chose the latter. The charred and ruined cities were rebuilt and the Imperial cult of Divine Claudius was moved to London, which now became the capital of a peaceful Romanised England.

CHAPTER 10

"Amber coloured hair…"

With a fanfare of cornets and rattling drums the acrobats shinned up the golden ladder and somersaulted from the top. They were a fine sight but Nero could not take his eyes off the beautiful woman next to him. She was the wife of his friend Otho, and her name was Poppaea Sabina.

"That husband of yours boasted too much for his own good. I can see why he did, but whatever happens now is his fault."

"I quite agree."

"Your hair is so glorious I might have to break into song! "

"That's why I go about so thickly veiled. I don't want to bring Rome to a stand-still."

"You do well to keep your beauty veiled. It should only be for the few. I feel I could rise to great heights in praising it. But your Otho is not a poet. He can't possibly do it justice!"

"He hasn't your way with words, but he does throw better dinner parties."

"Oh! You dare to tease me. But I shall make his dinners look like pig-fodder, and make you immortal too."

"The people love your songs too much. I can't have my 'glorious' hair on the lips of every tanner and costermonger in the street. Perhaps your Greek concubines* might appreciate that sort of thing..."

"Maybe Greek concubines aren't my style any more..."

"...I think you're a bad influence on my Otho. He's idle and dissipated. Needs something challenging to do."

"Mmm ...shall we send him off to govern Lusitania?"

It was 62 AD and the emperor was in love again. Poppaea's husband Otho, a lazy, extravagant drinking chum of Nero's felt increasingly like a gooseberry and was packed off to be a provincial governor in Lusitania

(now Portugal). A new rhyme appeared on the walls of
Rome:

"Why does Otho live an exile's life?
Because he dared to sleep with his own wife."

Acte, Nero's faithful concubine, retired to a sumptu-
ous villa to make way for Poppaea. There were other
changes, too. Burrus, the commander of the Praetorian
Guard, died – of natural causes. In his place, two joint
commanders were appointed to the Praetorian Guard:
Faenius Rufus, who had managed the corn supply effi-
ciently, and Gaius Ofonius Tigellinus, who, like Nero,
loved horses and wild parties. He was thought to be a
cruel, greedy man – the worst kind of influence on the
Emperor.

Without Burrus, his trustworthy old colleague,
Seneca felt alone. For many years now he had been
a power behind the scenes. It was impossible to wield
such influence without becoming rich even though
his personal habits were frugal. He had enemies who
envied him, and Nero was now less willing to listen to
his advice; it was time to retire; his health was poor.
Philosophy, he said, would be his mistress now. They
exchanged flowery compliments and Seneca offered to
hand over his accumulated wealth to his former pupil.

The unspoken thought was that if he gave it freely now he wouldn't have to be murdered for it later – for naturally he would be expected to leave most of it to Nero in his will.

Nero badly wanted the money. His extravagance was causing problems with the treasury, but he knew that if he accepted, everyone would guess why the offer had been made. He did not wish to appear a money-grabbing tyrant. So Seneca continued to be rich but kept away from court.

The people Agrippina had put in place to fortify her son were slipping away. It only remained now for Nero to get rid of his wife Octavia. She sat demure and neglected in the Palace, the last relic of his mother's controlling zeal. This chilly marriage had produced no heir. Divorce was common enough in those times, but to divorce an imperial princess, so loved by the people, was something else again.

"If you want to divorce her, give her back her dowry," Burrus had replied when Nero broached the subject. By this he meant that Nero's marriage to Octavia had been crucial in making him Emperor. If he divorced her he should hand the empire back to her as well. But now Burrus was dead, and Poppaea was pregnant.

It was necessary, since the people loved her, to blacken Octavia's good name. So Nero accused her of having an affair with a flute-player. But Octavia's slaves were loyal. Even under torture some of them refused to speak against her.

"My lady is cleaner – every inch of her – than your filthy mouth!" screamed her maid Pythias as she spat in the face of her interrogator. Finally, however, enough slaves had confessions wrung out of them. Octavia was divorced and banished to a country estate.

The Romans rioted – outraged at this cruel treatment of the most high-born woman in the empire. In the confusion, a false rumour that Nero had recalled Octavia back from exile sent them wild with joy, which was almost as fearsome as the riot. The army was sent to restore order.

"What are you going to do about it?" hissed Poppaea. She was trembling with rage and fright. "Shall you have the scum on the street dictate your choice of wife?" She didn't fancy being torn limb from limb by the mob should Nero lose his nerve. Already her statues were being smashed to pieces.

But Nero had become more ruthless, possibly under the influence of Tigellinus. He had recently ordered the deaths of two men whose only crime was to have carried the blood of Augustus in their veins. Rubellius Plautus and Felix Sulla had been quietly in exile, one in Gaul, the other in Asia, when, with very little explanation, their unoffending heads were cut off and sent back to the Emperor. The desire to see severed heads on plates is an odd one. They didn't look good after a journey of several weeks. But in a world without photographs or death certificates it was difficult for an assassin to prove in any other way that he'd done the job properly.

As ever, Nero decided to turn to Anicetus to carry out his dishonourable plans. Anicetus was the Commander of the Fleet at Misenum; He had helped plot Agrippina's "shipwreck", and he now swore on oath that he had been Octavia's lover, and that she had planned treason against her husband. She was sent under armed escort from her country estate to the island of Pandateria; and within days an execution squad arrived.

Octavia was only 23 and had harmed no one. The soldiers bound her with cords and cut open every vein, but terror stopped her blood from flowing. To speed things up, they put her to soak in a scalding bath. It was odd to die like this in a cloud of steam surrounded by strangers. The blood of the Caesars, that superior liquid, which should have entitled her to a life of ease and luxury, was staining her tunic a deep crimson. The soldiers' faces had the bored indifference of the boys who sat by the tubs in the cloth-works, waiting for the scarlet dye to "take". This death, so far from anyone who loved her was cruel. But at such times ancestors were a great help. She thought of their deaths on battlefields all over the Empire. They would not permit her to shout, however unbearable the pain.

She died at last and the soldiers cut her head off and sent it to Rome for Poppaea to gloat over. Twelve days later, Nero married Poppaea. It was said that to keep her skin soft she bathed in the milk of 500 recently foaled she-asses. If this were the case, she must have smelt very cheesy. But maybe Roman noses were deadened by the vapours of the "*Cloaca Maxima*", (the Great Drain), and the many open sewers of the city. Poppaea became a style queen; the perfumeries of Rome vied with each to create an auburn hair dye, as all the fine ladies now wanted coppery hair like Poppaea's, and a special face-cream was named "Crema Poppaea".

In the following January a daughter was born: Claudia. Nero's joy was boundless. "She shall have the title Augusta like her mother."

"But My Lord, a newborn baby with a name of such reverence?"

"Yes. Claudia Augusta... And we shall have a new Temple of Fertility in Rome. But in May the baby died. Nero wept long and loud over the tiny creature. He declared her a goddess and appointed a shrine and a priest. He never had another child.

CHAPTER 11

"Fiddling while Rome Burns..."

A dry hot night in July 64 AD. The dust had settled on the day's races and the Circus Maximus was quiet under a full moon. In the seedy shops under the arches a spark leapt. Whoomph! Flames licked and gobbled, splitting barrels of sticky wine, caramelising vats of honey, turning to ashes the charts of astrologers, sizzling the priceless pots of ointment "that cured everything", and buckling, in its fierce heat, the instruments of torture used by dentists. Soon the flames crackled triumphantly over the tiers of wooden seats, showing no respect for rank: commoners' seats, Knights' seats, Senators' seats, and the Emperor's grandstand. The fire roared up the Palatine and the Caelian Hill.

Nothing could stop it. Rome lit up the sky. Caught in the warren of streets, people ran round in circles. Some leapt to their deaths, trapped at the tops of blazing tenements. Some struggled to help old people and children in the narrow alleys. Others knocked over everyone that stood in their way. Wherever people ran for safety, they found more walls of fire hedging them in. Those who managed to escape with their lives got as far as the outlying fields, then threw themselves on the ground in despair, realizing they might be better off dead.

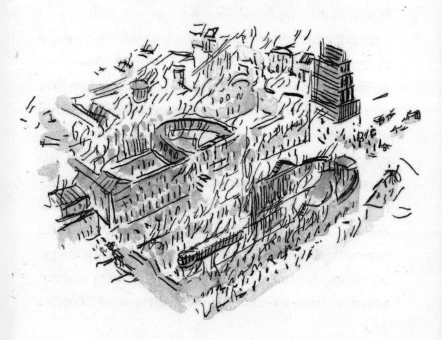

Nero hurried to Rome from his holiday villa at Antium. He set up emergency shelters all over the Field of Mars and in his own Vatican gardens. He gave out free food and drink. He cut the price of corn to a sixteenth of its usual price. Demolition gangs tried to clear open spaces and cut off the fire. After six days it seemed to have run its course, but then mysteriously started again and this time hurled its fury at Rome's most ancient temples and public buildings which were stuffed with treasures from all over the empire.

In the course of relief operations, Nero took a few moments off – and sowed the seeds of a legend. "Ah the terror, the beauty of flames!" he declared, "Let's go to the roof to get a better view. Bring my lyre!" He struck up a chord and sang some choice lines from "The Sack of Troy" in Homer's *Iliad**. The plundering and burning of Troy was vivid to all Roman imaginations. It was painted on Roman walls and written up in countless poems. Probably no educated Romans could glimpse a city in flames without seeing Troy, and in seeing Troy they saw the distant origins of Rome itself. Aeneas, the remote ancestor of Romulus who had founded Rome, was a Trojan prince who fled the flaming ruins with his father on his back and his son at his side. What Nero now saw was too great a temptation for someone as dedicated to drama as he was. Those little black figures running against an amber sky offered a backdrop and lighting effects such as no scenery painter had ever equalled. He seized the moment. People thought it heartless and inappropriate to sit there singing in the middle of it all, and so the phrase "*to fiddle while Rome burns*" was born. It sums up Nero's attitude to life. He would always try to wedge a little music and poetry between himself and unpleasant realities.

Now, in spite of his efforts at fire fighting and food distribution, he came to be regarded as the cause of the fire. This was unlikely to be true, but ugly rumours flew about and some fire fighters said they had been hindered by mysterious gangs of thugs with torches. Even though Nero had suffered the loss of his own newly decorated palace, people still said he had started the fire to clear the ground for new building works. The anger of the people was a serious cause of alarm. Nero felt himself to be in trouble and looked about in a panicky way for scapegoats.

He decided on the Christians. They were just what he needed. Christianity was then a new religion. Jesus Christ had been crucified in Judaea thirty years before, and since then the Church had spread rapidly through the Eastern Empire. The Saints Peter and Paul had both preached in Rome and there was already a flourishing Church there. There were probably Christians in Nero's own household. But it was early days and they would still have been regarded with suspicion. Their talk of universal love and their claim, at the Eucharist* to be "eating and drinking the body and blood of Christ," would have made many people think they indulged in sexual orgies and cannibalism.

The historian Tacitus* called Christianity a "deadly superstition". He said they were punished "not so much for setting Rome alight as for their hatred of the human race." This was probably because the religion had a wide following among the poor, who had every reason to hate life itself. Those who lived in miserable poverty in Nero's day looked forward to the second coming of Jesus and the end of the world in an all-consuming fire. This was thought to be due very soon. St Peter had written: "Beloved, think it not strange concerning the fiery trial which is to try you... but rejoice!", while St Paul had urged his congregation to "make of your bodies a living sacrifice". It was easy to misunderstand such mystical language.

The first to die in Nero's campaign of persecution were perhaps willing martyrs*. They were followed quickly by others less keen to die, whose names had been extracted under torture. The manner of their deaths was peculiarly unpleasant and farcical. Victims were dressed in wild animal skins and torn apart by dogs, or crucified, or dressed in "shirts of pitch" and lit up as torches to illuminate night time races in the Circus. Although the Roman mob usually delighted in bloodthirsty spectacles, the sight of writhing Christians failed to amuse them. On the contrary, fickle and unpredictable as always, they pitied the martyrs and felt disgust at the Emperor's cruelty.

In the meantime, Nero began the task of rebuilding a new fireproof Rome with strict rules. New buildings were made of stone, not wood, and had large spaces between them to stop fires spreading. Corpses and rubble were gathered up and dumped in the Ostian marshes. Romans, deprived of their old cool dark alleys, now complained they were blistered by the sun.

CHAPTER 12

The "Golden House"

In the midst of the debris and the blackened ruins, Nero longed to create something beautiful. His grandest ever project, he decided, would rise like a phoenix from the ashes. He started to build a palace and pleasure gardens that would devour a vast portion of land in the very heart of Rome. This was not a popular move, as it robbed the poor of places to live. It would be called the *Domus Aurea*, the Golden House.

A mile-long arcade led to the entrance-hall in which stood a colossal statue of the Sun God, with Nero's face. From here, the Emperor stepped into his private park. There was a huge lake with a jetty, and fishing-boats.

Even the haughtiest carp might feel privileged to be caught in Nero's personal fishing net, which was made of gold, meshed with purple silk. Fleets of swans glided over the water like quinquiremes* in full sail. Flamingos, peacocks and partridges strutted along the shores among ornamental hamlets and pavilions. There were vineyards and pastures with curly-horned cattle and goats, and copses full of chattering goldfinches. Hares hopped and fawns nibbled by rustic shrines in shady groves. Doves perched round the rims of fountains, cooing and dipping their beaks in cool water.

Stepping into the house you would see the same sights, but now painted and framed in fake windows on the shell-white walls. In between these dainty landscapes, nymphs, fat Cupids, and mythical beasts cavorted on dangling vines or airy balconies. These frescos were painted by Fabulus, who always turned up for work dressed, not in some labourer's tunic, but in his best bleached toga; to maintain the dignity of artists, he said. Nero thoroughly approved.

The banqueting hall was a great novelty: an octagon of brick-faced concrete, created by the architects Severus and Celer. Daylight poured into it through a hole in the cup-shaped roof.

"How do I know what time it is?" Nero prompted his guests.

They looked puzzled.

"Do you not see how the roof revolves? At midnight it returns to the same point as twenty-four hours before. Every two hours we run through a sign of the zodiac."

"Miraculous, My Lord! Like one vast water clock!"

Nero loved gadgets. In the bathrooms you might take your choice of salty or sulphurous running water. (Sulphur springs smelt foul, but were considered then, as now, excellent for the health.) The music room boasted the hugest water organ the world had ever seen. It made unearthly fluting noises as slaves paddled a treadmill and air whooshed through its pipes. There were dining rooms with carved ivory ceilings and gem-studded walls. Dinner guests lolled on couches decked with Babylonian embroideries. They sipped Caecuban wine from Myrrhine goblets, and roses might be showered on their heads. Sudden sprays of perfume from secret pipes cause gasps of surprise and pleasure.

"At last I can begin to live like a human being," preened Nero.

"I have a passion for pearls," he said to Petronius, his writer friend, whose good taste he and all Romans regarded as the last word.

"I have decided to strew my little love dens with them. Girls and pearls!"

Petronius would approve, for Petronius had said that wives were out and girlfriends were in. One day Petronius complained, "I can't seem to dine anywhere these days without skidding on sodden rose petals."

The next day, roses were out and cinnamon was in.

CHAPTER 13

"Hell guides your feet…"

After such extravagant building work, it was hard to balance the accounts. Nero owned huge numbers of properties, cornfields in Tunisia, villas all over Italy, even a tile factory in Britain. Much of this came from legacies, since it was the custom for rich people to bequeath the emperor half their goods when they died. Otherwise their families would suffer from his displeasure. But in spite of these vast resources Nero was heading for bankruptcy. As usual the reality was disguised by superficial splendour. The coins minted in Nero's reign were the most artistic and accomplished Rome ever produced. But as the coins increased in detail and artistry, so their actual worth in metal was reduced.

The art stamped upon these coins had a purpose. It was to remind the people what a good Emperor Nero was. They showed exquisite pictures of the goddess Ceres* – who symbolised corn rations – or the harbour works at Ostia, or the Market rebuilt after the fire, to remind people how much care the emperor took of their food supply. This was the reason why the common people loved him. But at the same time the portraits of Nero's face on the head side of the coin show why the ruling classes couldn't stomach him. The deep-set eyes, protruding chin, chunky neck and bohemian haircut with its flowing layers of curls arranged by his famous barber Thalamus, gave him a vulgar "show-biz" look. This was the style adopted by charioteers and actors. Sober, respectable young men of the upper classes wore their hair cropped short. It would be similarly shocking if the British prime minister were to get himself up as a rock star for official photographs.

It was typical of his mad frivolity that when a dubious-looking African appeared at court claiming to have discovered the cave where Dido Queen of Carthage* had buried her treasure, Nero based all his hopes of an economic recovery on this unreliable traveller's tale. Instead of reining in his spending sprees – as he should have done – he sent off an expedition with spades, to dig up the hidden hoard, and continued, meanwhile, to pile riches on his favourites, and throw lottery tickets into the crowded Circus. It was fun to see people scrabbling for the prize, which might be a farm, a block of flats, a seaside villa, or some jewels or slaves.

In 65 AD it was time to celebrate the second Neronian Games. This was the moment when Nero decided finally to make his public debut in Rome by entering the Singing Competition. Until now, he'd only performed privately. The festival planners worried about what people would think. They tried to prevent the scandal by offering him the prize of "Victory in Song" and "Eloquence" in advance of the contest. "I would rather win the honour by merit." he replied, "I don't want special treatment, and I have faith in the good taste of the judges." So with a touching show of nerves, he took his turn along with the other contestants, and once he'd finished, got down on one knee, held up one arm in salute and awaited the judges' all too predictable verdict. Visitors from the provinces were shocked to see their Emperor in this unbecoming posture, and so were the notables of Rome, but they joined in the cheering, glued to their seats. Their faces ached from smiling.

Rome had by now become a dangerous place where only the most foolhardy expressed their true opinions. The games were intended as a cheering distraction from a very unpleasant business that had been rumbling on for months – The Pisonian Conspiracy, as historians call it, involving a plot against Nero's life. Nero's right-hand man, the vicious Tigellinus who commanded the Praetorian guards, had set up rings of informers everywhere to report even the slightest signs of disloyalty to the emperor. Satirical remarks, sneers, fidgeting or lacklustre applause would all be noted. The dreaded charge of High Treason had been revived, and not even the brothels or public lavatories were safe any more since spies were everywhere.

This had caused the ruin of Seneca's nephew Lucan, a famous poet. Roman lavatories were very public and sociable; they had neat rows of seats – stone slabs with circular holes cut out of them and water running along a drain underneath. One day Lucan had been enthroned on one of these seats. He gave vent to a long loud fart, and the temptation to make a joke suddenly became too much for him. He quoted an apt line from one of Nero's well-known poems: "You might suppose it thundered 'neath the earth..." There should have been a ripple of laughter but instead, everyone got up abruptly and hurried away. The informers did their work; Nero got to hear of it and Lucan's promising career was irreversibly blighted. Then he became caught up in the Piso plot, and was finally obliged to commit suicide.

The comic actor, Datus, risked his life when, one night in the theatre he had uttered the lines: "Goodbye Father, goodbye Mother", and mimed the motions of drinking and swimming. Everyone tittered as they thought of Claudius and Agrippina. Then when he came to the lines: "Hell guides your feet," he pointed towards the gallery of Senators. Nero had such a soft spot for the performing arts that he was merciful and only exiled the man. Even tyrants have a sense of humour.

But Hell was, indeed, where the Senators were bound. From the moment that Tigellinus, commander of the Praetorian Guard, had got wind of a plot against the Emperor's life, the famous conspiracy of Piso was unravelled bit by bit in a series of cruel interrogations that lasted for many months. It is uncertain now whether the plan had been to put Seneca on the throne, or a younger man, the good-looking charmer Gaius Calpurnius Piso. Fifty-one people were eventually charged: nineteen

Senators, seven Knights, eleven officers and four women.

The first person to be tortured for information was a freedwoman called Epicharis. When the word got about that she'd been arrested, the other conspirators panicked. Women were not supposed to be brave, and the men were sure that even at sight of the gruesome torture rack she would tell everything she knew. They started trying to save their own skins by informing against each other. People who had been in on the conspiracy themselves, actually ended up interrogating other conspirators, or taking them death warrants. As Tacitus* put it, "A fatal spell of cowardice was on them all." They should have had more faith. Epicharis was conspicuously brave. After hours of having her limbs torn on the rack she gave nothing away, and while they were carrying her on a stretcher back to the cell for further questioning, she managed to hang herself with a strip of clothing.

Nero helped conduct the investigation himself. "Why did you break your oath of loyalty?" he asked Subrius Flavus, one of the main officers involved. Flavus didn't mince his words. He knew he was going to die: "Because I hated you! I was as loyal as any of your soldiers as long as you deserved affection. I began hating you when you murdered your mother and wife, and became a charioteer, and lyre-playing Rome-burner!"

The beheading took place beside an open pit. Flavus pronounced the pit to be neither wide enough nor deep enough, and contrary to army regulations. But he firmly held out his neck: "Be resolute," he said to the Tribune.* His head was cut off in two sword-strokes.

Many deaths followed. It was the privilege of the well born to be allowed to commit suicide, rather than be executed. Piso cut his veins and left a will bequeathing everything to Nero – as well as a letter praising the Emperor's beautiful voice and skill with the lyre. Piso loved his young wife and wanted to save her.

Seneca died like a philosopher. The centurion* would not allow him time to write his will so he turned to his friends and said he bequeathed them instead the comfort of his example – a virtuous life. After pouring a libation* on the altar of Jupiter the Liberator, he and his wife Paulina slashed their wrists. But Nero sent soldiers to save Paulina's life. They bound up her wrists and she lived a few years more, a pale relic of her famous husband.

Seneca's nephew, the poet Lucan, who had never been forgiven for his irreverent joke in the latrines, cut his wrists and bled to death slowly – quoting his own poetry this time.

The Consul Vestinus had not been involved in the plot, but had been foolish enough to marry a beautiful noblewoman called Statilia Messalina, without realizing she was Nero's mistress. Vestinus was having a dinner party with friends in his splendid mansion overlooking the Forum, when a squadron of guards arrived. He rose at once without a word, retired to a chamber with a physician, cut his veins and climbed into a warm bath. His guests were kept under guard for most of the night, staring at each other across the cold remains of the feast – until Nero laughingly said they had paid a high enough price for their dinner with the Consul and allowed them to totter away into the cold light of dawn.

Rome was filled with the smoke of funeral pyres. As if the executions were not enough, a hurricane swept through Campania and a plague carried off thousands. In the middle of all this, Poppaea died, possibly from a miscarriage. She had always said she would hate to grow old and lose her beauty. Nero was grief-stricken. He had the body embalmed with spices, burnt up a year's supply of Arabian incense, and had a mask made from her face which he wore when acting female roles. After a while, he married Statilia Messalina, the new widow of Vestinus.

The poet, Petronius, that clever lazy man who set the tone for the smart set, managed a stylish suicide. He may or may not have been involved in Piso's plot, but either way Tigellinus had marked him out as a man to get rid of. As soon as Petronius understood that his position was hopeless, he cut his wrists – but not before smashing a priceless vase which Nero had hoped to inherit. Then he had them bound again from time to time to delay death a little.

Meanwhile, he chatted, dined, slept, woke, gave presents to some slaves, had others flogged, made up silly verses, and, finally, sent to Nero, under seal, not the legacy or the grovelling flatteries he might have expected, but a long list of the Emperor's most undignified sexual frolics, together with the names of his partners.

CHAPTER 14

"His Excellency Nero wins this contest…"

In 66AD Nero organised one of his finest pieces of pageantry. A slight blot on the horizon was the rebellion in Judaea and Galilee – but in an empire so large there must always be trouble brewing somewhere. It was, after all, what the Romans saw in Rome that counted. Today was a day when plots and executions could be forgotten, and Rome's greatness remembered. The Consuls, and Senators in crisp white togas were seated in tiered ranks round the Forum. The guards' cohorts stood at attention, spears and shields gleaming in the sun. Humbler people were packed into every possible space along the Sacred Way, from the Basilica Julia to the

Velian Hill, and even perched on Triumphal Arches and temple roofs. Nero sat enthroned on the rostra* near the Senate House in front of the Temple of Concord, splendidly draped in cloth of gold. All eyes were fixed on his visitor, the turbaned Tiridates of Armenia. Only the flapping of flags in the breeze broke the expectant hush as Tiridates ascended the ramp and prostrated himself at Nero's feet. Nero stooped, raised him by the hand and kissed him. Then he replaced the turban with a diadem. This meant that he, the Emperor, was making Tiridates a king. In return, King Tiridates handed over to Nero an assortment of sons and nephews, including the son of his brother, the King of Parthia. Parthia was a mighty empire in the East, which had a long history of enmity with the Romans and had not been defeated by them. For Nero this day was the fruit of careful diplomacy. He had ensured peace between Parthia, Armenia and Rome after years of fighting, and managed to make his compromise solution look like a military triumph. This was no mean achievement.

"You have done well in coming here in person to enjoy my presence," Nero intoned. "Your father did not leave you this kingdom; your brothers, though they gave it to you, could not guard it for you; but this is my gracious gift to you, and I make you King of Armenia, in order that both you and they may learn that I have power both to take away kingdoms and bestow them."

The crowd shouted "Imperator!" and Nero led his guest to the theatre, which had been gilded with a fine sheen of festive gold. A purple awning decked with golden stars kept the sun off. To the astonishment of the visiting king, the Emperor raced in his chariot and played the lyre. Later they dedicated a laurel wreath on the Capitol and shut the double doors of the Temple of Janus, to show that all war was at an end. The rejoicing lasted many days. Tiridates' journey home would take nine months. When he left, with cartloads of costly presents, he promised to rebuild his capital city and rename it "Neronia".

Now Nero planned an artistic tour of Greece. Only the Greeks, he said, knew how to appreciate good music. He left his Greek ministers in charge at Rome and pointedly failed to kiss the Senators goodbye, as was the custom. This was a dangerous snub. He took with him on the journey his new wife Statilia and a beautiful young man, a eunuch called Sporus whom he "married" ceremonially when he got to Greece. "Pity Nero's old man didn't marry that kind of wife!" they quipped at Roman dinner parties when they heard of his "wedding".

The Greek Festival organisers made huge efforts to keep Nero happy. He was a winner wherever he went – like his glorious role model Alexander the Great. He couldn't imitate Alexander's lust for war but he planned to conquer by the gentle arts of music and song. At the Olympian games he competed as a charioteer, driving a ten-horse team. He was hurled from his chariot and had to be hauled back in, half fainting. It didn't matter that he hadn't completed the course. He still won, and the judges were handsomely rewarded. In lyre-playing and tragic-acting contests he won no less than 1808 prizes, defeating the finest musicians of the day. "His Excellency Nero wins this contest," he proclaimed each time, "and bestows his crown of victory upon the Roman people and the inhabited world, which is his."

One place he didn't visit on his tour was Athens. It was too closely connected with myths of the Furies pursuing Orestes after he murdered his mother. In Corinth, with great pomp and ceremony, he started digging a canal through the Isthmus – the finger of land that joined the mainland onto the Peloponnese. Using a golden spade he scooped up a great clod of earth. A deafening blast of trumpets hailed this mighty deed, and while he mopped his brow with a silk handkerchief, 6000 Jewish prisoners took up where he left off. But they only got a fifth of the way. Nero's successors abandoned the project and it waited nearly 2000 years to be completed. In fact, the Corinth Canal, now in constant use, was not opened finally until 1893.

In November, 67AD Nero stood in the middle of the stadium at Corinth and declared Greece free. This was his ultimate expression of love for all things Greek. Greece, conquered by the Romans three hundred years before, had, over the centuries, re-conquered its conquerors. Great art, literature and philosophy were greater in the end than mere force of arms. Yet now Nero had vanquished them again with his voice, in a single-handed, bloodless victory. The Greeks had reorganized their sacred festivals so that he could sing in all of them. They had beggared themselves scraping together prize money. The Greeks understood great art. They loved him and he loved them. And since he was carting off wagonloads of priceless paintings and statues from their temples, he felt he could afford to show his gratitude. The speech he made, amid patriotic cheers, is still preserved on a bronze tablet in the town of Karditsa, Northwest of Athens: "Unexpected is this gift, men of

Greece, though perhaps nothing can be thought unexpected from munificence such as mine. It is more than you could dare to ask for ... Other emperors have freed cities; Nero alone a whole province." This impractical act of generosity assured Nero undying popularity in the East. But Rome needed the money from Greek taxes, and the gift was cancelled soon after by the next emperor.

Nero's happy visit to Greece was interrupted by news of another plot, in the army this time. A series of ill-judged and panicky executions followed. He summoned Corbulo, one of his best generals, and as soon as the poor man reached the port of Corinth, he was told to kill himself. "*Axios*" muttered Corbulo, before plunging a dagger into his heart. This means "deserved" in Greek. He didn't mean that Nero's suspicions were justified, but that he was a fool to have come. Two other commanders of the legions in Upper and Lower Germany were also summoned and made to kill themselves. Nero had made a fatal error in punishing these men without a trial. Now no one felt safe anymore.

The Greeks were hailing Nero as the "New Apollo" and "Zeus the Liberator", but back in Rome the corn supply was failing, soldiers' pay had got behind, money was short and the upper classes were smouldering with resentment. Nero's minister, Helius, urged him to return home urgently, so he decided to dazzle the people back home with a Triumph. Roman generals had always been accustomed to celebrate their victories with a military procession along the Sacred Way to the Capitol where they dedicated their captives and spoils of war to Jupiter. The difference now was that instead of prisoners clattering through the streets in chains, squadrons of battle-scarred legionaries, and long lists of conquered territories – which is what the upper classes would have liked, the Emperor's chariot was decked with garlands, bay leaves and wild olives. His only "captives" were a few "vanquished" lyre-players, his own teacher Terpnus among them. The Emperor rode along in a purple cloak that glittered with gold stars, enjoying the shouts of "Victor of Olympia! Augustus! Nero Apollo! The one and only all-victorious!" He dedicated his wreaths in the Temple of Apollo on the Palatine hill, but afterwards had them brought to his own bedroom.

CHAPTER 15

"What an artist dies in me!..."

In 68 AD, after his Triumph, Nero retired to Naples, the Greek-speaking city where he felt more at home. In March, on the anniversary of his mother's death, some bad news arrived. Some legions* in Gaul – which we now call France – had broken their vows of allegiance to the emperor. The commander who had raised the revolt had a name that even the stoutest heart might find a little daunting: *Vindex*, which, in Latin, means "Avenger". As the news reached Rome a fresh breeze of liberty blew through the fetid streets. The whispered slogan "*Vengeance and Freedom*!" began to be heard everywhere.

Even the commoners in Rome were angry now. Food was short. People took liberties with Nero's statues. Someone draped a sack over one of them with a note saying "you deserve the sack!" (Death by "the sack" was the traditional Roman punishment for parricides – people who killed close relatives. They were tied up in a sack with a viper and thrown in the river Tiber to drown.) More insults were daubed on the walls: "This is a real contest for once, and you are going to lose!"... or "Your crowing has awakened even the cockerels!" This was a witty pun: The Latin word *Galli* meant not only cockerels but also Gauls, the people who were now in revolt.

Nero veered between panic and ostrich-like denial. When he heard that Vindex had said he played the lyre badly, he was shaken to the core. He visited his friends to ask what they thought of his lyre playing. Wasn't it outrageous what Vindex had said? Yes, they replied, it was hard to believe the petty spite of the man. What an unforgivable slur!

But the revolt was spreading. When news came that Galba, the governor of Nearer Spain, had declared against him, Nero fainted. He hurried back to Rome and called a meeting of advisers, but even then couldn't bring himself to concentrate. An inventor had arrived with a fabulous musical instrument – a new-fangled water organ with a treadle and finely carved hollow pipes. Nero left his council and rushed off so that he could inspect this marvel and experiment with its eerily beautiful notes. His ministers were at their wit's end: "My lord we have a crisis on our hands! We must beg you for a moment's attention".

"Yes, yes... but let it wait till tomorrow. I've just remembered there was a play on at the theatre I particularly wanted to see."

So Nero rushed off again, this time to the theatre. But there seemed to be no respite anywhere. The loud applause an actor was receiving nearly drove him mad with jealous rage. If it weren't for those wretched Gauls he would step on to the stage right now and show them what great art really was.

"They only clap him to the skies because I'm not there," he muttered. "That man is taking advantage of my present troubles. What a nuisance to be so tied up just now!"

He cheered himself up with eating and drinking, and stumbled out of the dining room on the shoulders of friends. "Do you know," he drawled, "what I shall do when I get down to Gaul?"

"What will you do, My Lord?"

"I'm going to step out, unarmed, in front of the enemy. Then I shall weep and weep. They'll be softened, and remember their loyalty."

"Of course they will, My Lord!"

"Then the next day I shall stroll among my joyful troops shouting paeans* of Victory. I must start composing them now."

The provinces were plunged into confusion. Galba joined Vindex, and so did Otho, the governor of Lusitania (Portugal). But Verginius Rufus commander of the legions in Upper Germany, after months of dithering finally marched south in support of Nero and defeated Vindex at Vesontio, (now Besançon in Southern France). But in the meantime the legion* of Clodius Macer had revolted in Africa. No one close to Nero had faith in him any more. He had lost all sense of reality. Even his Praetorian Guardsmen quietly gave up on him.

Where could an Emperor hide? Egypt? Parthia? Greece? Nero's thoughts became increasingly mad and disconnected: "I could go to the Forum dressed in black and beg the people's pardon. I can live by my art even if I cannot be Emperor. They love my singing... but perhaps for now it's a good idea to leave Rome... go quickly and prepare my fleet at Ostia".

While he waited he nodded off and fell prey to hideous dreams. He was steering a boat across the bay of Baiae. In the dark a woman's strong hand took the tiller away from him – it was his mother's; then his wife Octavia seemed to be tugging him down into a black pit, and winged ants swarmed over him; his favourite horse turned into an ape, except for the head, which whinnied a tune; the doors of his family mausoleum* burst open, and a hollow voice boomed: "Enter, Nero!"

When he awoke, his guards had disappeared, so he decided to flee on horseback with Phaon, one of his freedmen, three servants and Sporus his faithful eunuch* – whose face reminded him of Poppaea. Before leaving he grabbed an old cloak and put a handkerchief over his face. He was in such a rush that he only had one shoe on. "Let's head for my villa, My Lord, between the Salarian and Nomentan Ways. Then we'll think what to do next," said Phaon.

"Yes, yes ... I need a peaceful place to think," mumbled Nero. They passed a barracks and heard voices. The guards inside were loudly insulting the Emperor, promising him all kinds of mischief, and hailing Galba the Liberator. Nero huddled shocked under his cloak. It was a thundery June night. Lightning flashed across the sky. A rider galloped towards them. "It's the hunting season! Everyone's out looking for the Emperor..." he shouted as he passed.

At that moment Nero's horse reared at the smell of a corpse by the roadside, and the handkerchief fell from his face. He hastily clapped it back on again, but an old army veteran, standing by the road, muttered an oath and jumped to attention. Nero's companions bustled him away, but they knew now there was no hope of escape.

They came to a dark lane leading off the road, and dismounted. After plunging through some prickly bushes and a reedy bog, they reached a half-derelict house. While his companions started digging a secret way into the cellar, Nero scooped some water from a pool and drank from his hands. "Nero's own special brew..." he muttered. He crawled through the tunnel into the secret chamber his friends had prepared, and flopped onto an old mattress where he soon became absorbed in pulling thorns out of his cloak.

Phaon rode back to the city for news. Nero felt hungry but when a slave offered him a hunk of grimy stale bread he turned his face away. He looked round the squalid cell and moaned, "Oh, how ugly and vulgar my life has become!" Sporus huddled beside him, pale and drooping. "Is it such a terrible thing to die, My lord?" he sighed. The other two attendants begged him on their knees. "Don't be taken alive My Lord! You cannot let that happen." Nero goggled at them with his pale sweaty face. Tears rolled down his face. "It's not time yet... Weep for me Sporus! ... I must have a grave. Start digging it now. I'll lie down here so you can measure me. Perhaps a few scraps of marble could be found."

A runner arrived with a letter from Phaon. "Emperor, you have little time," it said, "you have been declared a public enemy. If caught, you'll be punished *in the ancient style*." The *"ancient style"* meant being stripped naked, having ones head thrust into a forked stick and being flogged to death. Nero seized the two daggers he'd brought with him. Faint and trembling he ran his finger round their points. "Someone show me how to die!" he whimpered. He heard a far off rumble of hooves. A squadron of cavalry, with orders to take him alive, were galloping up the road. "Why can't I be brave?" moaned the Emperor, then, in Greek, "Oh Nero, this does you no credit, no credit at all ... Pull yourself together man."

The horses had stopped outside. "What an artist dies

in me!" gasped the Emperor. And with a clumsy thrust, he stuck the knife into his throat. Even as he did so a Centurion scrambled into the room. He wished to save the emperor for a more horrible death - the death which had been decreed "in the ancient style" – so he pulled off his cloak and wrapped it around Nero's neck to stop the blood from gushing out. "Too late. But what loyalty!" Nero was trying to say. But all his companions heard was a painful hissing noise. His eyes were glazed and bulging; terrible to look upon.

EPILOGUE

Nero was buried in his family tomb on the Pincian Hill. His first girlfriend, the faithful Greek concubine Acte and his two old nurses gave him a lavish funeral. Their loyalty shows that Nero still inspired love in those who were humble and didn't threaten him.

The historians Suetonius and Tacitus, writing a generation later, paint a dire picture of him because of the destruction he wrought upon the upper classes. They cared less about the lower levels of society. But for ordinary people, the ones who weren't writing the history books, most of Nero's reign was both peaceful and prosperous. As long as they had bread to eat they didn't mind too much if he played and sang in public. It was the corn shortages, and his wildly unbalanced behaviour at the end, which cost him their loyalty. And if anyone rejoiced at his death that rejoicing was short-lived, as the whole empire plunged into chaos and blooshed.

At the start of his reign Nero had hated signing death warrants, but the years of power, and the ever-growing fear of treachery, brought out a streak of cruelty and madness. With such a vicious family background, this is hardly surprising. Nonetheless, to start with, and when he had good advisers, he was both efficient and enthusiastic. He had a great appetite for life and poured energy into schemes for the general good, promoting festivals, public buildings, engineering works, trade and exploration, and replacing war by diplomacy. But his persecution of the Christians ensured him a particularly bad press in the following centuries as Christianity came to dominate the western world.

"Nero will always be missed by the riff-raff," sneered the next Emperor, Galba, who, six months later, was murdered by his successor Otho. In the three months that Otho was Emperor, he restored some of Nero's banished statues. They had once been friends after all, and loved the same woman. But then Otho was murdered in his turn and another old friend of Nero's, Vitellius, became the third Emperor in what later came to be called "the year of the three emperors". Vitellius paid tribute to his former friend by calling for "one of the Master's songs" at a banquet. Little of Nero's verse survives: half a line about thunder, another about doves' feathers ruffled by the wind, and the words "amber-coloured" which he used to describe Poppaea's hair.

Nero continued to be loved in the East. In the course of the next twenty years, three different impostors claimed to be him, and received enthusiastic support. People couldn't quite believe he was dead. Like Elvis Presley or King Arthur in years to come, he had acquired legendary status. For Christians, on the other hand, Nero was the Antichrist, the "Beast that was, and is not, and yet is." In the 12th century Pope Paschal II demolished Nero's tomb because he heard crows cawing in a walnut tree nearby and took them to be demons serving their master. The Church of Santa Maria del Popolo now occupies that spot.

One wing of the Golden House has survived and can now be visited in Rome. For centuries it was buried under the foundations of Trajan's and Titus' Public Baths. The Flavian emperors made it their boast that they restored Rome to the Romans. Nero's delightful boating lake was drained and became the site of a vast place of entertainment, the Colosseum, so-called because of the colossal statue of Nero, which used to stand in the antechamber of his villa. By the Middle Ages people had forgotten the place ever existed. But one day in 1480, some diggers tunnelled in through the roof. At first they thought it was an underground cave. They lowered themselves down on ropes with rush torches. With shouts of astonishment they saw the beautiful frescos on the walls. It was their first vision of a colourful antiquity, a wonderland of Fauns, dolphins, lyres, leerinf faces, and leafy temples. Artists came and copied them. Creatures with horns and wings and curly tails were unleashed upon the walls of Renaissance Europe. The Neronian style of wall decoration, which now became all the rage, was named after the supposed "grottoes" from which it had emerged, and thus a new word entered the language – "grotesque" – for all things monstrous and fantastical.

GLOSSARY

Augustus – This word in Latin means *majestic,* or *worthy of honour.* It was bestowed as a title of honour upon the first Eperor of Rome, whose actual name was Octavius Caesar. (see below) Afterwards he was known simply as the **Emperor Augustus.** The title *Augustus* was always added on to the names of subsequent emperors as well. The month of August is named after the first Emperor Augustus.

Caesar – This was originally the surname of the Julian family to which Julius Caeser the famous soldier, statesman and and writer belonged. After he was assassinated, his great nephew, who was also his adopted son, Octavius, (later the first Emperor), took on that surname. It then became, like *Augustus,* an honorific title given to all emperors. It is from this word that we have the German imperial title of Kaiser, and the Russian title of Tsar. People called Nero *Caeser* much as we would call a king *Your Majesty.*

centurion – the rank of officer in the Roman army.

Ceres – a goddess of corn and fruit, the origin of our word cereal.

Consuls – were originally elected in pairs to serve for one year as leaders of the Senate and commanders of the army. During the republic the 2 consuls had supreme authority. Under the emperors the consulship became merely an honorary post lasting 2-4 months. The Emperor might serve as consul himself or propose other candidates.

Capitol – A hill in the centre of Rome overlooking the Forum on which stood the most important and ancient temples.

Carthage – A country in North Africa on the Mediterranean coast facing Sicily.

Carthaginian – a native of Carthage. (See Virgil's Aeneid for note on Dido Queen of Carthage.)

Concubine – a kept mistress or lover, often a slave obliged to share the master's bed but without the privileges of a wife.

deification – the turning of a human being into a god. Julius Caesar and Augustus (see above) were both declared gods after their death, as well as Claudius. (Tiberius, Caligula and Nero were not).

eucharist – giving of thanks, hence meal of sacred bread and wine.

Eunuch – a castrated male. They fetched high prices as slaves. The priests of the goddess Cybele, a popular cult in Rome, were eunuchs.

Faun – a lustful woodland god or demon, half-animal, half-human, companion of **Bacchus** god of wine.

Field of Mars – originally the Tiber flood plain used for army exercises, later covered in monumental buildings, porticoes, and theatres. It was here that Nero built his famous Baths.

Forum – the main square and meeting place in a town. The Forum Romanum, (ie the Roman Forum) was the heart and centre of Rome where foreign kings were received, speeches made, and the courts of Justice and the Senate met.

The Furies – 3 infernal goddesses of vengeance who tormented mortals for their sins, also called Eumenides or "the kindly ones".

Hecate – mysterious three-faced goddess of the crossroads, associated with sorcery and the ghost-world. Offerings of dog-flesh were put out at crossroads to keep her sweet.

Homer's Iliad – a long poem in 24 books, narrating the Trojan War, ie. The wrath of Achilles and the 9 year siege and destruction by the **Greeks of Troy**, also known as Ilium Troy was a rich city on the Mediterranean coast of Asia Minor, (modern day Turkey). Probably composed by the poet Homer c. 800 BC. Staple reading for all Roman school boys. See note on Virgil's *Aeneid*.

Infernal Regions – those places', supposedly beneath the earth , to which people went to after they died.

Janus – An ancient Roman god of entrances and beginnings. The month of January is named after him. It was a tradition in Rome to shut the doors of his shrine only when Rome was at peace with the world. This rarely happened.

Jupiter – the father of the gods who had his temple on the Capitol. Corresponds to the Greek god Zeus.

Legion – the Roman equivalent of a regiment, it consisted of 10 cohorts of foot-soldiers and 300 cavalry, adding up to a total of 4200 - 6000 men.

Libation – pouring out of wine in honour of a god.

Litter – a luxurious chair with an awning over the top, carried along on poles by eight strong slaves, and often provided with glass windows or curtains.

Martyr – (comes from the Greek word "witness") those who die to prove their faith.

Mausoleum – a stately burial chamber for grand families, so called because of Mausolus, a King of Asia Minor whose funeral monument, built by his widow in the 4th century BC, was one of the 7 wonders of the world.

Minerva – Roman goddess of Wisdom, trade guilds, handicrafts and flute-playing, (corresponds to Greek Athene)

monarchy – a system of government in which there is one supreme ruler, (usually hereditary).

Paean – a hymn of praise or thanksgiving for deliverance or victory.

Palatine – a hill in the centre of Rome overlooking the Forum on which the Imperial Palaces were built. The word *palace* comes from the name of this hill.

Quinquireme – a ship or galley with five banks of oars.

Rostra – platform or stand for public speakers in the Roman Forum which was decorated with the beaks (ie prows) of captured enemy ships. Rostra in Latin means beaks or snouts.

Satyr – a lustful woodland god or demon, half-animal, half-human, companion of Bacchus god of wine.

Senator – a member of the Senate, a government assembly whose decisions had the power of law. Its authority was very much limited under the emperors.

Suetonius and Tacitus – 2 Roman historians who wrote a generation after Nero, the two main sources on Nero's life.

Tiber – the river that ran through Rome and came out at the sea in Ostia.

Virgil's Aeneid – Long poem written (in 12 books) by Virgil during the reign of Augustus. Tells the legendary adventures of the Trojan hero, Aeneas, who flees burning Troy, (see note on Homer's *Iliad*) sails all over the Mediterranean, falls in love with and then forsakes Dido Queen of Carthage, (whose treasure Nero hoped to dig up), because his destiny is to found the dynasty that leads to Rome. Like the *Iliad*, staple reading for Roman school children.

Quiz

*After you've finished the book, test yourself and see
how well you remember what you've read.*

1. Nero's surname at birth, Ahenobarbus, means:
Bearded chicken
Rusty spear
Bronze beard

2. As his father was dying, Nero's nurse urged the boy
to:
Catch his last breath with a kiss
Run away and hide in a cupboard
Sacrifice an ox to the gods

3. After his father died, Nero was brought up by:
A barber and a dancer
A butcher and an athlete
A baker and a lion-tamer

4. When Nero's mother Agrippina married Emperor
Claudius, Nero was:
Adopted and given a new name
Banished to a small island in the Mediterranean
Told to join the army and see the world

5. His tutor Seneca taught the young Nero how to:
Ride a horse and chariot
Play the guitar underwater
Be a good public speaker

6. Emperor Claudius died from eating a deadly mushroom and:
Being tickled by a poisonous feather
Holding in a fart too long
Lack of exercise

7. Optimus mater, the first password that Emperor Nero gave to the Praetorian Guard, means:
An optional matter
The best of mothers
My good mate

8. Seneca wrote a play mocking the Emperor Claudius called:
'The Pumpkin-Eaters'
'I, Claudius the Pumpkin'
'The Pumpkin-ification of Claudius'

9. Nero found his wife and step- sister Octavia to be:
Delightful and loving
Emotionless and dull
Intelligent and ruthless

10. In the early years of his reign, Nero was popular because:
He gave away corn to the people
His public performances were wonderful
He was a good role model for the young men of Rome

11. To entertain the people of Rome, Nero arranged fights at the Field of Mars between gladiators and:
Wild boars
Guinea pigs
Old women

12. Nero loved dancing, but was not very good at it because:
His legs were thin and he had a fat belly
He had a bad back
His tiny feet made him fall over

13. After Agrippina escaped from a shipwreck he had planned, Nero sent:
A bunch of flowers to show his concern
Reporters to write about the terrible accident
Soldiers to murder her as she lay in her bed

14. When Nero wanted to be a charioteer, to protect his body against injury he would drink:
Pig snot in lemon juice

Dried boar's dung in water
Spider's webs in honey

15. In 61 AD a new challenge to Roman power emerged in Britain. She was:
Queen Elizabeth I
Queen Cartimandua
Queen Boudicca

16. Because Nero was bored with his wife Octavia, he:
Exiled her to Britain
Had her murdered in her bath
Sent her off on a round-the-world cruise

17. It was said that to prepare for her wedding with Nero, Poppaea had a bath in:
The milk of 500 female donkeys
The urine of her 20 maidservants
The sweat of 10 pregnant pigs

18. When Rome was swept by a dreadful fire in 64 AD, Nero:
Burst into tears
Burst his pants
Burst into song

19. Nero's Golden House, the Domus Aurea, was:

A simple villa in the countryside
An elaborate complex in the heart of the city
A skyscraper development near the port

20. When Nero went into hiding, after much persuasion
from his companions, he:
Ran away to Egypt
Gave himself up and begged for mercy
Committed suicide

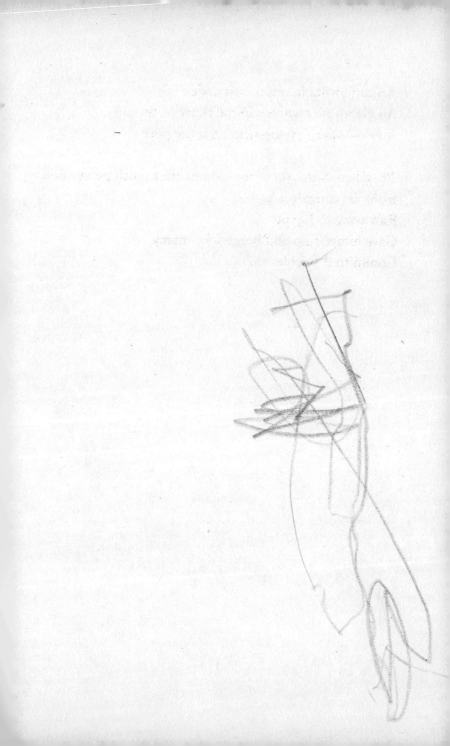

Noonie Minogue is a book reviewer and writes regularly for the *TLS* and the *Tablet*. She is a member of the Primadonnas' Party Quartet, in which she plays the cello and Spanish guitar. She lives in London with her children. This is her first book.

Backlist

1-904095-76-3

1-904095-84-4

1-904095-85-2

1-904095-80-1

1-904095-86-0

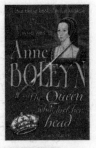

1-904095-78-x

1-904095-61-5

1-904095-65-8